MY STORY....

THE ORPHAN REGIMENTS

Victor Lorenzetti

Trafford rev. 08/08/2018

Trafford PUBLISHING® www.trafford.com

North America & international
toll-free: 1 888 232 4444 (USA & Canada)
fax: 812 355 4082

ABOUT THE AUTHOR

I was born in 1926 in rural Walpole, Massachusetts to a blue collar family, one of four siblings. Economics of the day were poor and living standards were not very high. My father was an Italian immigrant, my mother born locally.

World War II for the United States started in 1941. When I turned 18 in March of 1944 I was drafted into the service joining two older brothers already serving. In my story you will see I moved quickly getting trained, served overseas, becoming a prisoner of war, liberated and honorably discharged. What I endured left scars that will never heal.

Lastly, I should note this work is my only attempt at writing a book. It is hoped the readers will not look for literary flair, grammatical elegance, impressive sentence structure and the like. Instead, focus on the story content with the terrible conditions of war and survival and try to imagine yourself in my shoes and those that suffered with me.

DEDICATION

Dedicated not only to my fellow former 42nd Infantry Division prisoners but also the approximately 90,000 other former American prisoners of war in Germany, both living and dead, that endured similar hardships.

To my two older brothers, one Air Corps the other Navy who, like me, were lucky to have survived the war. They served their country well and were honorably discharged. Both are now deceased.

ACKNOWLEDGEMENTS

I would like to express my gratitude to my daughter and illustrator, Camille Murphy, for her devotion and talent in her preparation of the drawings and cover designs for my book.

Further, it is worthy to note of the patience shown by my wonderful wife, Jean, for the countless hours consumed during the writing and endless additional time for finalizing this work.

To all those in the family around me for their encouragement not to give up and finish this small but important piece of my life.

THE PRISONERS LAMENT

Within our humble homes a call was heard
It was quite strong by sound and by word
The problem it seems was a nation in plight
And needed to muster our young to the fight
Soon our turn came as we entered the ranks
And moved right along with our rifles and tanks
As we trained and prepared to enter the fray
Our lives were at risk but that was the way
How could we know we'd face bitter cold
Cause a soldiers place is to do as he's told
The regiments planning did not fare that well
Which caused our cold bodies to march into hell
We faced a big battle without much to show
Knowing full well we'd be dealt a harsh blow
The enemy's strength was something not known
Our meager resistance was away quickly blown
Their armor was moving with force and with might
The action against us now plainly in sight
When brought to the village how many would be lost
For when the trucks left told;" HOLD AT ALL COSTS"

So this was our mandate and we dared not bend
Our weapons soon emptied as we now faced the end
There would be no help our leaders revealed
We will end up this way as our fate was now sealed
The enemy moved quickly and surrounded our crew
Causing plans to be made then to help save the few
So away we were taken to await our sad fate
If any help came now it was already too late
They marched us some distance over frozen terrain
Not up to this task our boots brought us much pain
Herded into our campsite certainly something not nice
Our wracked bodies soon hosted a home for the lice
So now we must struggle to survive the ordeal
For finally when it's over perhaps a good meal
In the meantime we exist to a prisoners tune
And only dream this life's hell will end real soon
The Author

Contents

1

INTRODUCTION TO A NEW LIFE

I am a former prisoner of war (POW) of World War II, was held in Germany and this is my short and difficult story. For those unaware of the extent of Americans becoming prisoners this was no small matter. Details shown later will indicate that in Europe alone about 94,000 of us were captured and incarcerated as German prisoners.

It was bitterly cold in early January of 1945 at our assigned positions here in Northern Alsace. Our three green infantry regiments were spread thinly along a thirty mile front. It appears our leaders didn't comprehend the tactical situation fully, resulting in constant and even baffling shuffling movements. There was considerable wrangling concerning defensive strategy in the upper echelon of command explained later in the story. Around us the snow was already more than knee deep and the evening sky had that stormy look that more could be on the way. Strong cold winds caused a chill to the bone agonizing our seemingly constant move-ments. My squad had already been moved around the surrounding area several times in the past two weeks for unknown reasons. Operational circum-stances resulting from this quickened and seemed to suggest the enemy might be poised to strike some-where soon. But where would that idea come from? German patrols had been showing themselves and they seemed to move around at will with little con-cern. Little by little though, over the past two weeks their presence was on the increase. This, by itself, could have been a red flag. Still from headquarters, all advice filtering down to us indicated we'd face no more than enemy patrols. German strength, we were told, was being moved north to a large opera-tion in Belgium. But suddenly and from out of no-where our only physical link to the distant remain-ing company command post ended as our trucks began moving away. As the last supply truck pulled away from our strung out squads spread around the village our lieutenant in charge was told to; " HOLD AT ALL COSTS". The stage was now set, for what happened soon thereafter positioned us for our ordeal. Our fate was now sealed with no way out. ....But wait, I need to slow down and stop here, then go back, as I'm getting way ahead of myself and...............my story!!!!!!!!!

To put this adventure into some perspective due to my short time military span I thought I'd start a few months earlier than my actual army time. By doing this I wanted to set a tone of what my life was like before the ordeal I was to face. The war years were unpleasant anyway for just about everyone but we could only deal with our immediate surroundings and those we grew up with. So this story will chronicle the events from high school (seems like a good place to start) to my experiences in the service, army life as a recruit, movement to basic training camp, to divisional formation, overseas, combat, capture, confinement, liberation, discharge and return home. To say my experiences were compressed in time would be an understatement.

My accounting of this ordeal will seem, at times, to be un-patriotic and maybe a bit of sour grapes or even un -American, but that was not the case at all. The bitter taste from my experience and perspective was always, I felt, justified. For the military's actions it will be quite unflattering at least as I and other POWs saw it. Later in the story from a referenced book most other fellow POWs in their accounting seemed to agree. The same bitterness I carried for a long time resulted from the seemingly unplanned and uncaring methods of fighting this war. Maybe wars are supposed to be screwed up and I just didn't know it or gave it much thought. If they are, I'm sure it would not be publicized openly. Up until this time my only experience with the war was what we saw in the movie news and heard on radio. When the Japanese bombed Pearl Harbor in December of 1941 I was only 15. For the next three years the main source of war news was as above. Our other news feedback was through my two brothers already serving but that was skimpy at best. Everyone tended to believe any news shown to them. As my story unfolds I will try to highlight the many movements placed on me and my comrades under combat conditions, the hopelessness and the resulting confusion leading to my capture. These difficult to deal with events were put into print as will be shown later.

Our rifle platoon company was placed into a no win situation and by some measure might even be called "sacrificial". Whoever was planning our movements either didn't know the true circumstance or, if they did, couldn't do anything to help us and so the worst for our green regiments happened. In their scheme of things our vulnerability with its potentially huge losses was, ,most likely, not even a consideration and so was played out by our commanders. This was a desperate time in the war with the Germans preparing for what might be called their last big offensive. Their preparation for this might not have been fully understood and with faulty intelligence yielded confusion. Germany's intelligence, however, must have seen something worthwhile in our sector perhaps setting an opportunity and as we now know prepared to act.

To sum it up, the Germans correctly spotted the extreme weakness in our location and moved against it with strength. Whether they were just fortunate or did their intelligence point out the arrival of our inexperienced division is lost in time. All along this section of the Rhine, maybe about 30 miles worth, raw and green recruits like myself were overwhelmed by superior forces and many dead and prisoners resulted. Prior to our moving to the combat areas, it was our understanding we would be moved to a section that presented no immediate threat and with no large enemy forces to speak of. Bad information as it turned out and with it, our fate. A factual statistic of our operation; almost all of our divisions prisoners for the whole war were captured in their first month of combat. But, in the final analysis, and as ordered, we held our ground until we had nothing left to hold with. Many were lost, but those that survived, myself among them, paid the price almost to the extreme. Those survivors, like myself, would have to endure extremely harsh living conditions unimaginable by those not there.

On the home front my hard working immigrant father had a heavy burden.---- We were first generation Americans and out of four siblings the three males were now in active service after my induction. The only girl in the family, my sister, was to join in the family's grief and could only hope the war would end soon and get us home safely. The daily news covering the war with large casualties being reported was for them, at best, a painful reminder to watch and bear. I was born (there were four of us) in a rural town in Massachusetts but the family moved to Boston when we were all quite young. The city offered more employment opportunities. I grew up in the city and our neighborhood like most was very close knit. Boston, probably like most cities, was ethnically diverse so we grew up with many nationalities. Diversity was something unknown at the time, never spoken about, and a non-issue. Actually, we made fun of our differences sometimes, had a laugh or two, and no one was offended. Sadly, in today's world this is no longer allowed since we must be " politically correct". Everyone got along nicely as we were equally poor and differences didn't mean anything. It seems the collective poorness actually provided bonding that made us closer and better neighbors and friends. We knew just about everyone and all news, good and bad, moved quickly. The last thing any wartime family wanted to see was uniformed military knocking on their door.

Since WWII there have been many war stories covering all branches of the services; land, sea and air. And ,of course later, we were also provided several movies and TV on POW's in an effort to show the country and world a look into that kind of sad episode. I don't believe there have been any POW experiences from a personal first person perspective and from a before and after dialog. What I experienced may be considered a bit unusual for my story of these Army adventures from beginning to end was quick and lasted only 18 months.

None of the POW stories I'm aware of portrays the horrific happenings as seen through my eyes. I am witness to death, dismemberment, utter destruction, endless human tragedy and the futility of war. Furthermore, I don't remember any war movies showing the terrible planning as in our case nor the devastating physical and psychological results. That is something you don't advertise and not good for our Government's public relations. I have, since my return and after many years, have asked myself what was the point? Much of the war was recorded on film but I don't remember seeing any coverage of POW's, how they were forced to exist or when being liberated to show their emaciated condition of skin and bones. I and those around me, when liberated, were not asked to be photographed. It seemed to me that most coverage of that time period was focused on concentration camp prisoners and their ordeal. With these pictures made after the war the Germans, now our friends, certainly should have looked like monsters. Pictures of us should have been included as well. Our captivity treatment proved beyond any measurable doubt the Geneva Convention was a worthless paper document. About as worthless as the United Nations is today. Perhaps this is another one of our Government's cover ups as we were to find out later there have been many with maybe more to be exposed in time when they are ready.

The war ended in Germany and Japan, and with the ink hardly dry and the bodies of the dead not quite cold yet, saw our Government go crazy and started rebuilding efforts. Our former enemies were now our good friends. Over much time the same kind of wars we fought with England, Spain, Vietnam, and Korea and we do business with all of them. So what was this war, any war, all about? Someone once said; "war is good business" so maybe that's the real answer; wars are for the business community. What a system, blow them up real good then let American businesses rebuild. It would seem wars are a useful economic tool. The price, however, was the enormous human losses in excess of 280,000 young Americans, the wounding of many more, and literally millions from other countries. Americans are constantly told that we fight in foreign countries to preserve our freedom at home. When I was eighteen I guess I believed it but as I got older it does not somehow come across as believable. In my mind there were serious doubts that connecting those dots made me feel safer.

My short stay in the service was directly as a result of my age. It was late in the war and I did not turn 18, draft age, until March of 1944. At the time I had two older brothers already serving since 1942. Rather than wait to get drafted I felt let me try something where I might have a say in my near future but it was not to be. My attempt to join the naval air corps was not accepted as I will explain later. At that time in the war producing manpower for the services had only a single focus.

2

FINISHING HIGH SCHOOL

At the time of my high school years the war had been on since December of 1941.Everything around us reflected the difficult years that had been going on. The story starts in my high school years 1940 to 1944 when I graduated. I was in a technical high school and we had a good assortment of machine tools (some quite old) that became useful for making small mechanical items helpful for the war effort. I don't think it was publicly known that in a small way we were helping the war. Not far from us in another town was an arsenal making some kind of guns or cannons and where our parts went. What they were actually making was not for the public to know. In the early 40's which was a tough time economically, my high school like so many in Boston, looked like a manufacturing plant and was, in fact, located adjacent to a huge railroad yard. The school and railroad yard have been gone for quite a while and the whole area has changed dramatically after the war years.

Even so, with its bleak and run down appearance the teachers of that time period were totally dedicated, discipline was the rule and getting out of line was not tolerated. When anyone got out of line the teacher was allowed to give corporal punishment by whacking our hand with a stick. In today's pampered society schools are not allowed to dispense any corporal discipline. Furthermore, our factory like appearance would be condemned as unfit for study. For us, we didn't give it much thought as that was the norm of the day and the way things were. It would be safe to say our entire class was from working class families. Schools for the privileged did exist in our day but was out of our reach . Even our class size was about 35 to 40 students, large by today's standards but again pretty typical for the day.

High schools then in Boston did something that was probably unique in the country. In either the last three or four years of school it was required for all males to take drill instruction. All were to wear army style uniforms including leggings and shoes and to carry a mock rifle. Class time for marching practice was set aside the same as going to the gym. I think it was in the spring that a city wide parade was held with all high schools and their bands being represented. Because this was an annual event it was widely publicized in advance and drew a large audience to the parade route. This marching also provided a form of competition among the schools and judging committees made selections and presented awards. Eventually this activity died out and ended in later years for reasons I can't remember.

Graduation during these years was low key, held without much fanfare and quickly forgotten. My school was all male by decree. Girls were excluded because it was unheard of then for females to enter the mechanical trades. For fairness, schools for girls only were provided as well. In that time period, females were usually trained for home economics, secretaries, and to become wives, mothers and homemakers. Circumstances of the war caused a sobering effect all around us. Besides that, most working people had short salaries and lived a week to week existence with few frills. Before I turned 18 in March of 1944 I had ambitions to become a navy flier. I'm not sure why I came up with this idea but I think watching the newsreels of war footage and the rotten conditions of ground warfare convinced me I should take my chances in a different branch. The fact that my brothers one in the navy, the other in the air corps did not escape me. It seemed to me, and I was quite convinced at the time, that anything would be better than getting shot at on the ground. Wartime footage showing soldiers up to their ankles in mud, hiding in bombed out houses, crouching near fences and building to keep from getting shot was not a pretty picture.

The idea of being a pilot somehow had a feeling of status like a movie star and placement among the elite. War movies, maybe without realizing it, tended to glamorize pilots, especially fighter pilots, and make them out to be heroes and possibly role models. For movie makers, this was a form of propaganda but to me as an eighteen year old tickled my ego. So, in my decision I completely ignored the war news and the large losses suffered by the Air Corps fighting in Europe. This group, especially those flying bombers suffered large losses as a percentage of those involved. My high school was a good one for pilot training for we were well versed in math and other technical subjects and I was certainly young and also in good health. At the time, my two older brothers had earlier enlisted in July of 1942 as did many of the young men of the neighborhood. .

When I got the inspiration (good a word as any) to be a navy flier I had to fill out some papers like ; copies of school grades, permission from my parents and statements from the Police Department showing that I had no record. The navy denied my application but I was never given a reason even though I asked. Many times I wrestled with this rejection, some right away, and some in later years. Was I looked upon as not acceptable because of social status? I'm sure that wasn't the case but the idea for this did appear in a film made in later years. I wish I was smart enough at the time to join the Navy or some other suitable branch of the service. As I learned from the circumstances explained later, I probably wouldn't have been allowed this either. In my mind, and from the terrible war newsreels, anything would have been better than being on the ground. Certainly the war was still on and you would think new pilots were needed as replacements. Announcing losses for all services seemed to be a daily thing. The real reason for my rejection started to become quite clear to me later in the story when I went to Camp Gruber. It was late in the war then (although no one could have known how long it would last) .The Army was taking men from many military programs, wherever they could get them, and putting them into the infantry. What the Army was doing was providing replacements for the high infantry casualties of both the European and Pacific campaigns. Infantry losses by the numbers were huge when compared to the other services and their branches. The full impact of the depth of these losses were summed up as; "The infantry, by far, absorbed the greatest percentage of casualties: 80% of Army killed in action. Riflemen equaled 68% of an infantry division's manpower, but accounted for 95% of it's casualties.***

My school, a technical one (there were two in the city) , and being all male graduation services were less formal, without cap and gown, simple and very low key. Being in the war years with it's visible hardships further reduced the joy of graduating. I don't think my family was in attendance. We received our diplomas in a quick informal ceremony, dressed in typical street clothes, extended handshakes and good luck to each other and went on our way. As you might expect, all the graduates like myself, were at 18 or would quickly come of age and could expect soon to become war material. I knew it would happen, so naturally I assumed they had to come up with the same thinking. I was not aware of percentages but I believed this late in the war the largest share entering the military ranks were draftees. Government regulations required all males to register for the draft upon becoming 18 years of age.

*** *Excerpt reprinted by permission of the VFW Magazine, May 1995*

3

ENTERING THE ARMY LIFE

Soon after graduation in April of 1944 I was inducted into the Army on 27 May and sent to Fort Devens, Massachusetts near the New Hampshire border. Things were moving right along; turned 18 in March and in the Army in May. Even though we were draftees it was here we were sworn in and had to take the oath of serving. After this we could officially be called " GI's" . I was not sure how this thing of being called GI's for us grunts developed but the GI stood for Government Issue. Still a little strange expression, but typically American. With my induction meant all male members of my family were now in military service and all could be put in harms way. Later in the war I believe an effort was made to limit the exposure that one family should bear so as not to lose all male members.

This was an old camp still in use since World War I. Even though it was April, It was still cold, barren, somewhat isolated, not a nice place but a proper introduction to army life (ugh). The camp was only about 60 miles from my home but we had to stay on base probably to get acclimated to military discipline. We were being trained to make the transition from civilian to Army life. I think I spent about three weeks there for what was called indoctrination and processing. I sometimes thought that expression "processing" made us new recruits feel like chickens moving along a conveyer belt. I can't quite remember if we were allowed to visit home before being sent to our next charming location but I think we were. Our stay here lasted until near the end of June then I think we had a couple of weeks at home. Besides seeing family again the home front was still the same. Not much else to do except talking to friends and neighbors (too young or too old for service) and reading up on war news. The war was the main topic on everyone's mind so discussing it became a daily occurrence. Movie houses in those days routinely showed newsreels covering the war and other news. While trying to adjust to Army life my thoughts were always on the war in the Pacific and in Europe (because of my brothers) and the knowledge that the much talked about huge invasion of Europe was nearing.

News of the time gave much coverage of the impending invasion of Europe as the beginning of the final assault against Hitler. This was to be a costly invasion no matter what so much was done to confuse the Germans. Months were spent on the planning for this assault so mixed signals were deliberately sent many times. It was hoped the selected invasion landing site would be kept secret as long as possible. How well this was done remains a matter for historians. The actual assault was labeled D Day and occurred on June 6, 1944 on the French coast called Normandy. However one looks at it the casualties were enormous.

Once in the military it was difficult and infrequent to communicate to my brothers and our home. My oldest brother, Rico, assigned to the landing crafts in Europe would again soon be put in harm's way big time. Up to now he had made it safely after having being involved in several invasions in Italy. He later told us he thought the worst was at Anzio in Italy. Far away in the Pacific my brother Ted in the Air Corps (as it was then called) was flying missions from some unknown and unnamed island. As we found out later, he was both a radio operator and gunner; common duty on smaller bombers. His group flew B25s over jungle terrain and most always stayed just above tree top level to avoid anti-aircraft fire and radar contact.

We were issued uniforms, a duffel bag, overcoat, underwear and shoes and a set of metal tags called "dog tags". These tags were mandated to be worn at all times around the neck on a beaded chain and were our identification (ID). On these would be our name, religious preference, a serial number, and a funny looking notch at one end. Just about all of us wondered what the hell was the notch for? After awhile when curiosity got the best of us we inquired as to the purpose of the notch from cadre non-coms (army talk to describe non- commissioned officers). There was a reluctance initially on their part to answer but eventually did so hesitatingly. Finally with a very straight face we were told that if and when you got killed this dog tag would be placed into your mouth with the notch locking onto the teeth so the body could be identified and properly registered for the burial detail!!!!!!! Knowing that certainly improved our morale and boosted our comfort level.

When clothing was issued the Army must have had a method for selecting sizes. It seems the men with large frames would be given clothes that would be tight and those that were thin given clothes that would be too big. When these men inquired why the choice of size they were told everything would be fine during basic training. It was truly amazing the Army was right; those that were overweight lost weight and the thin ones gained. Not too sure why or how our activities molded us to a good fitness but it seemed to work. The training was intended to be harsh and it was and we grumbled a lot but the reality is that physically it made us really fit and we looked and felt better for it.

For those young men, even older ones, who had a strong sense of modesty this new life style would quickly open their eyes for all of us had to rapidly adapt to communal living, like it or not. For me, I was already exposed to some of this community living from my high school days. Another thing that prepared me was visits to clubs with indoor swimming pools run by the city. Boys and girls each had separate clubs where the boys were mostly always naked. I don't what the girls did in theirs. Bathrooms in our high school had urinals stretched along a wall where all we did was line up in a row with no privacy. You could always depend on a wise guy making jokes about someone. This frequently resulted in a fight breaking out. In these city neighborhoods having to fight was to become a ritual while growing up. In the camp nobody was coddled (like many in today's society) and complaining was not listened to or given much attention. One of the things learned quickly was if one had a complaint, "to go see the chaplain". It was a loose military joke and not really intended to be taken seriously. The message here was a way to get the complainer to forget about it for no one would listen anyway. During my short stay in the Army the notion of complaining would be quickly swept away for it truly would not get anywhere.

All modesty was quickly dispersed as we moved into barracks with many other men, had to eat as a group, and best of all had to go to the bathroom (#1& #2) and showered in a very open space arrangement. Privacy was not on the list and was not even close to being a consideration. Much of the army's potty humor we were to learn resulted from many naked guys showering and toileting in a communal setting. Much was said about the pitfalls of being careful not to drop your soap while showering.

One of the important lessons we were to be taught (and would be carried over to other installations) was to maintain a code of discipline regarding our personal hygiene, appearance, and our assigned personal barracks living space. Army barracks were usually on two levels and everything, bunks and foot lockers, were out in open space maybe 30 to 40 per floor. No modesty panels were provided. Beds were to be made army style and hanging clothes was done in a specific way. Our shoes had to be arranged and aligned in a designated and orderly format on the floor . All shoes were lined up under the bed and dress shoes always had to be highly polished. It was each individuals responsibility to keep their area organized, clean and

was checked periodically by barracks officers sometimes wearing white gloves. The Army also had daily
dress code standards so we had to observe the post-
ings for " uniform of the day" on the bulletin board.

Economic conditions of the times at home was
poor for our family as well as most others around us.
With the war on, there was plenty of work and the
money was adequate for the time but little excess.
You could not always get what you wanted because
of shortages and many food items, gasoline, heating
fuel and other essential military necessities were under government controls and rationed. Soap was an
item of some importance because it contained glyc-
erin, useful in making munitions. When the size of
our bars of hand soap got real small all civilians were
asked to save them for collection. I forgot how this
was done but the pieces were collected and, I suppose, used for that purpose.

We didn't have all that much extra food at home
but no one went hungry. As a result, and not being ac-
customed to fancy food I became easily satisfied with
army chow (food) and what others did or thought was
of no concern. Daily activities were planned with
some classroom work and lectures on what we were
expected to do as members of the armed services.
Pay, as close as I could remember, was about $21 per

month and from that we had to pay for our service life insurance and a charge for our laundry was also deducted. That didn't leave much for personal items or for mad money when we had a chance to go into town. Later, when we learned about going overseas I arranged to send some money home as we prepared for overseas. It was explained that we would not have much need for money.

4

BASIC TRAINING FOR THE RECRUITS

From Fort Devens I was sent home for about two weeks. Time was spent catching up with the war's effect at home and how the neighborhood was coping. When with the family I had to get them to realize I may not have any more visits before going overseas. About mid- June I received instructions to report to a beautiful garden spot known as Camp Croft near the town of Spartanburg, South Carolina for three months of basic training. Travel was by train as the only realistic option. Good timing, I would now be exposed to the worst summer months. I am using the word "I" because not all of those inducted at the same time were being sent to the same place. As all of us found out quickly the army typically would build camps where it was unfit for human habitation (at least that was our take on it then as there was a need to inject some humor) so there we were out in the "boonies". At this time of year it certainly was hot and humid making it quite natural to sweat a lot. I got used to eating food I knew nothing about such as grits, black eyed peas, okra and catfish and which were local favorites. I was looked at strangely by the other northerners because I actually thought this kind of food was pretty good.

The people around us, good southerners, made us feel welcome and I will never forget their warmth, hospitality and the good Americans that they were. Although I liked the southerners I am sorry to say other northerners didn't share my feelings. Never did get to understand the ignorance of this and why some harbored such resentment. Some of those that did , I think, looked upon them as intellectually inferior because of their drawl. Who knows, maybe it was carry over from the Civil War. People we met in town would talk and move about in a slow manner. The perception was therefore all southerners must be slow. I sometimes defended this by saying if you lived where it was this hot then perhaps you wouldn't move so quickly either.

In 1944, Spartanburg was not a very big place but more of a typical and quiet southern town. Could even be called a little sleepy. Our camp was located some distance from town, had a share of swampy areas, had snakes, alligators, was hot, buggy and generally not too hospitable. Going into the summer season with high heat and humidity didn't help matters. On the plus side we were in farming country with animals, vegetables and many fruits most notably peaches. And yes when they ripened we took our share when out doing training exercises and tasted real good. Peaches from this area were large and juicy and mostly the type used for commercial canning. Georgia is the state most associated with peaches but we were not far from their state line.

Training life here was tough as I guess it was supposed to be. The Army personnel who lived on base and whose job it was to train us were called "cadre". Upon arising at the crack of dawn (usually in the darkness) we heard that ugly sound of the bugle known as reveille. We dressed quickly and then lined up outside in the company's street. They (the cadre) would make us slow jog for two to three miles ending up and directly going into the mess hall (military jargon for where you eat) for breakfast. You would quickly learn to eat whatever was put in front of you. But, if you were a little fussy and didn't eat then you were advised the next meal could be a long way off. In an effort to toughen us up for what we could expect later we often had to go on field exercises with rifles and full gear. An important part of these exercises was to show us how to use and eat prepared and packaged foods. Once overseas these prepared packages would be our principal food supply. For off base or overseas use the military developed a variety of canned and packaged foods. Us trench grunts were not considered royalty so eating out of cans was ordained as totally acceptable. There was little doubt that we would all be overseas and these foods would follow us there and be all that was available to us most of the time. Not a pleasant thing to look forward to but was a reality check to prepare us. We were politely being told to get used to eating cold foods and where taste was not a consideration.

Considerable time was spent doing marching and rifle drills outside under a hot sun. You can imagine how bad we must have looked for many of us had trouble knowing which was our right and left foot. I had no trouble doing this due to my high school drill training. Since these drills were considered quite important as soldiers it was done frequently. When you are forced to do something over and over, by getting it right sooner rather than later would help you to get inside and out of the sun quicker. A really smart thing to do during a South Carolina summer. After the first month we actually started to look like we knew how to march acceptably but a certain amount was still required no matter what. Marching was considered a natural part of Army life. The rifles of those days were really heavy and to say we were sweating our brains out would be an understatement. In the field we were told, and forced, to take salt tablets and get our water from what was known as a Lister bag. This bag was a large rubber pouch with bottom spigots hanging from a tripod. I believe the name comes from a physician Dr. Lister who created it and also became famous by name as the mouthwash " Listerine". Not the most pleasant thing to be drinking from but was better than water from our canteen which could get very hot in short order from being in the sun too long.

I was never sure of the ages of the recruits like myself. We came from all walks of life from all parts of the country and when assembled looked like a huge bunch of misfits or lost souls. Our company picture would surely make the Germans tremble. The sight of us new recruits as a group would give most people a good laugh. Army discipline was hard to take at first with many of us trying to avoid much of it but in time it started to sink in that the discipline brought us together as comrades. Our cadre had a job to do so complaints usually fell on deaf ears. Things that we felt were "chicken shit" like making our bed in a precise way, polishing and aligning our shoes under the bed, picking up cigarette butts outside (with encouragement from the cadre like;" all I want to see is asses and elbows), hanging our clothes properly and things like that. This was considered crap by many but over time proved to have some benefit; it was good for discipline and without realizing it, helped in our bonding. There was no way to know how many would be kept together and sent to the next assignment as a group. Asking our training non-coms didn't help as they usually said they weren't privy to any orders and I believed them. Their purpose in life was to prepare each group to be useful soldiers as they passed through the camp.

We were being trained to use standard infantry weapons including the Colt 45 sidearm, carbine,M1 Garand (which was to become our main weapon) , BAR (Browning Automatic Rifle) several machine guns and the Bazooka (used primarily against tanks). There was also a device called a rifle grenade that could be launched from the M1. An attachment to the rifle muzzle was fitted and a special bullet (like a blank) was required to propel it. For most of these we had to take them apart, clean, reassemble until a level of proficiency developed. It was constantly drummed into us that in combat you needed to make sure you had a weapon that could keep working for if you were in that kind of situation there would probably be no one to fix it except yourself. Along with this, a lot of time was spent firing these on a target range repeatedly and usually under a terrible sun. Besides being brutally hot we were lined up side by side firing a lot of rounds without ear protection. Not a consideration at the time.

This and other war noises, to come later, did cause me hearing problems over time. My deteriorated hearing later in life was diagnosed as Tinnitus, not a very well understood condition and a difficult to describe constant head noise. Even worse there is no recognizable treatment nor medical procedures available.

At the end of the training day and after we had eaten and taken a shower we finally had some time to ourselves. It didn't take us long to figure out where to go. That place was the post PX, (short for post exchange) where cold beer, snacks and personal items were available at reasonable cost. With our small pay and deductions there wasn't much left for treating ourselves anyway. There were times when we would get permission to go into town but that was mostly on weekends. Regardless of where we were, it was our responsibility to get ourselves back to camp, check in and be in our barracks in time for "lights out". A military ritual meaning you should be in your barracks or bed by that time. Getting to town and back was not easy for most of us hitch hiked and depended on the locals. I think there was a small bus service but the timing was not always adequate. Failure to make it back on time could bring on some form of punishment which, to me , seemed to delight the non-coms. There was always a number of dirty jobs around the base that needed attention and were gleefully assigned to the late arrivers. Once such an occasion arose where I was in a group that didn't make it back on time. My particular punishment assigned was to clean the huge fans over the stoves in the kitchen. A most unpleasant task in the summer time in South Carolina

Beer served in the camp PX was reduced in alcohol content to somewhere around 3.2% by Government decree. In the heat of a southern summer it tasted great and it was all we could get here anyway. On those occasions when we did go to town the beer was much stronger and it didn't take us long to find out about the local homemade booze called "white lightning". Those that made and sold it would find a way to get it to us. Illegal stills, definitely a southern thing, where the booze was made were abundant and popular in the rural areas. From what we learned Federal authorities made some effort to find them and shut them down but when that happened the moon shiners (as they became known as) would efficiently move to a different location.

Since I, and most of the others, were sent to this kind of training in the hottest part of summer it was considered among us we were being groomed for service in the Pacific and possibly even for the talked about invasion of Japan. As it turned out the very opposite happened and who would have guessed that many of us ended up in Europe and in one of the coldest winters on record. As we spent time together the men of our company realized bonding, without even suspecting it, was taking place as friends. At the same time and without openly discussing it we could not help but wonder what was in store for each of us, where we would be sent next and who would survive the war. We could not know that when the time came we were sent to different locations and not get to know where others went because of the Military's code of secrecy.

July, August and September, really hot months, seemed to pass slowly. Our days were long but not all the time was spent in the field for we had many indoor classes. We were lectured on military strategy, protocol, basics of the Geneva Convention (what a joke that turned out to be), map reading, basic navigation, foreign cultures, first aid, and best of all, the highlighting of awareness, behavior and consequences of venereal diseases. Films we were shown on that subject made our hair stand up and silently convinced us, at least for the time being, to keep our fly's zipped. These films became a favorite and constant topic of discussion and did become the basis for many jokes. After the initial shock watching these films they did get used for some humor and many laughs. But later, human nature prevailed, would rise above all and proved that our quick promises made to ourselves could be overcome when the right situation presented itself. What we saw would not be forgotten soon but did sink in as caution to be used.

Southern hospitality was alive and well in Spartanburg. On some Sundays many of the locals would treat groups of us to good home cooking by feeding us in one of the church basements. A most pleasant array of foods different from that of our mess hall. From this our morale got a momentary boost for we knew or certainly suspected the near future would be most unpleasant. War time rationing was in effect and noticeable around us but we were in a rural setting with farms and their produce and livestock was in good supply.

It was required to give us some training where basic navigation was implemented to find our way in the event we got separated from our unit. Platoon sized groups were assigned a leader, loaded onto trucks around midnight and driven to some remote spot several miles away. During the ride none of us was allowed to see where we were going for we rode inside of a closed truck. At our drop off spot our leader went over the training plan. Using only basic equipment like a map, compass, flashlight, water and a raincoat to cover us when map reading. Our assignment was to find our way back to camp on our own within a specified time period. We completed ours after getting sidetracked a couple of times in good fashion and our reward was a good meal for they kept the mess hall open all night for us and the others also sent out with the same assignment.

As we approached the final training weeks our thoughts focused on whether we would get a home leave and, beyond that, our next assignment. Just as we ended our stay, information came that yes a home leave was going to happen giving us about three weeks and orders would be sent during this time. No guarantee was given on the three weeks and we had to understand that. Our reflection on three months training was again in some sense like a production line; our group replaced one before us and as we leave another group would replace us starting the cycle all over again. Those training us (the cadre) by now must be used to this turnover and even if they wanted to show a connection would think it best to keep all contact impersonal. No matter how hard our training was or how hot it became there is still that gnawing feeling a piece of us will remain. Although our contact with other trainees was short we could not know if our paths would cross in the future.

5

GETTING HOME ON LEAVE

In 1944 commercial air travel was in its infancy, was heavily Government regulated for its military VIP's for the war, was very route limited and expensive so most of us peasants traveled by train or bus. Service personnel got a reduced rate (which we really needed on about $21 per month) but any amount was still too much. I don't remember what it cost me. Even so, it was all that was available to us so we made the slow trip home and were still thankful. I did give some thought to the possibility of hitchhiking home but many problems existed. There were considerable miles to cover and the roads and cars in 1944 left much to be desired. But the biggest factor was the unpredictability of how long it would take. A complete and uncertain question. Remembering I would be working against a military timetable made this unworkable. How long we would actually have at home was unknown for all we were told is we would be notified during this time. I hoped for at least the three weeks mentioned. Communication at this time was almost done entirely by

Western Union telegraphs in the USA but later when overseas done by what was called V-Mail.

Going home to our neighborhood in late summer of 1944 brought a sense of wartime reality. As expected, there were few young men to be seen; and visibly there were the even younger and older or those unable to serve for whatever reason. People at home tried to show positive attitudes but you could see that three years of war took its toll. Almost everything was rationed and there were many items not available and that was it. Everyone had to make do with what they had and for the most part there were not many complaints. It didn't take long to figure how could anyone really complain about going without, when nearby families were learning of sons being killed. Movies during the war were a big attraction and didn't cost much. It gave families a source of entertainment where not much was available and at low cost. Much of what was shown was intended to boost morale and patriotism. Stars of the day were portrayed to be helping the war in some way. Much publicity was made when a movie star joined the armed forces amid extensive photographic exposure. My take on that was typical Hollywood hype to show them doing their part. I can say the truth was they never carried a rifle or worked the trenches nor got in harm's way. For the most part it was public relations

stuff and to "entertain" the troops.   Besides showing two full length features, newsreels were shown,
were popular and gave extensive war coverage which
was not always a pleasant thing. There was so much
carnage from the fighting that there's no doubt films
for public viewing were censored. Other war news
appeared in the newspapers and heard on radio. But
the war was something one couldn't forget so all this
news was part of daily life and watched.

While at home I did manage to meet with neighborhood chums also in uniform and who happened to
be on leave at the same time. Purely a coincidence.
One of my close friends did find out that his older
brother, a fighter pilot in Europe had been killed in
action. What I most missed was not being able to see
or to know where my two brothers were and if they
were alright. All I knew was that my oldest one, Rico,
was with an Navy amphibious unit in Europe and the
middle one, Ted, was serving on B-25 bombers somewhere in the Pacific. All communication was done by
mail (slowly) but nothing else was available anyway.
By the time the mail was received many weeks had
gone by. On the plus side I did get to spend some
quality time with my father and sister and as many
neighbors as time allowed. In our neighborhood there
was a popular variety store that was very conscious of
the war effort because they had two sons in uniform.

The owners took as many photos that they could of all those serving and assembled a large display for all to see. Neighborhood casualties were given recognition on the photos as that bad news arrived.

The War Department courtesy of Western Union informed me that I was instructed to report to another one of the military's garden spots called Camp Gruber, in the beautiful hilly area outside of Muskogee, Oklahoma. I couldn't help but wonder how many of those I spent time with in South Carolina would also be sent here. It was next to impossible to try outguess what the military mind was preparing for me or others for that matter. We did what had to be done and made plans to try and get there on time as ordered. Train service wasn't always the best so if timing got to be a problem and we could account for our whereabouts we didn't usually get into hot water.

6

INTO THE HILLS OF CAMP GRUBER

The trip in late summer of 1944 from Boston to Muskogee by train took three to four (?) days. Train service for some reason seemed to be slow. There were times we had to change from one train to another and times where we were placed on sidings and just waited. I don't remember being able to get hot food but snacks were available on most rides. Comfort was not a high priority of that time period either. Keep in mind this trip was made only in coaches and any sleeping would be done in short stretches and usually sitting up. Part of the way I got lucky when there was space on the seat I could stretch out and lay down, sort of. As I traveled from the northeast to the Midwest I could observe the constantly changing terrain and landscape. Getting closer to my destination I could make another quick assessment; Muskogee, Oklahoma and the surrounding hills was indeed no garden spot unless you were a Native American.

Terrain was quite different from our New England areas with wide open spaces and, in general, a very barren landscape with hills all around. And different from our neighborhood there was sights not seen in the Northeast; an abundance of Native Americans living on local reservations but not confined to them. Later when allowed to go into town there were sights I would just have to get used to. These natives frequented the bars and were known to develop drinking problems sometimes causing problems. Something else I noted was not to many men wore shoes but seemed to favor boots. It dawned on me that this was considered cowboy country. So to us outsiders we referred to the area as " Indians and hills". If nothing else, this was a whole new experience for a youngster like me . Unlike South Carolina the weather here could be quite warm and even hot during the day but downright cold after nighttime took over. Weather here can produce ice and snow seasonably.

It was here that they brought in all the support groups so that together with us as infantry, a complete division was to be formed or so we were led to believe. These included artillery, tanks, heavy weapons, quartermaster, medical, communication, and I'm sure other groups. The camp officers were apparently given orders from higher up and set out to officially dedicate the formation as; "The 42nd Infantry

(Rainbow) Division". This same Division, the 42nd , also served in WWI. Now our training had a new focus; that as working together as a cohesive division rather than a rifle platoon, or again, so we thought. This story of mine will be top heavy in things being changed frequently and how it seems confusion was a commodity in good supply. From all this I wondered how widespread this frequent changing and confusion might actually be?

We were not being trained to make use of, let's say, artillery for example, how or why or when we could get their support when needed, or what to expect. Some platoons within the regiment were set up as "heavy weapons" which were; heavy machine guns, bazooka's, and, I think, mortars. There was also something called a rifle grenade that could be fired from our rifle. I don't remember being trained to use all of these but I think I was shown how to use the bazooka but didn't really spend much time practicing. Being familiar with the weapons could come in handy later if the one using it got shot or killed. Later in my story there would be a time when we wished for some of this "heavy " stuff and more but the powers to be could not offer any help.

It seems every area we went to has there own variety of moonshiners and the hills around Muskogee were no different. Again we could get "white lightening" Oklahoma style around the camp when we got a chance to go to town. These areas being quite western resulted in our having to listen to "Cowboy" music in the PX and local bars. The juke boxes had nothing else to play. We continued our training for about two months here but along the way the military pressed us into service in an attempt to try and root out the local moonshiners that set up shop in the surrounding hills. I never found out why us grunts would be used for this but I suppose we were available and cheap help. Besides, I didn't have any reason to go after them but had no choice. Making this booze required a "still" which had to be fired up and this in turn would create a plume of white smoke that rose in the air and would give away their location. On windy days the smoke was not so noticeable. These people were quite savvy, however, and had their own communication system so when a raid was coming their operation shut down quickly and they would be gone by the time anyone arrived. Moonshining was illegal so I guess the local law enforcement had to make it look like they were only doing their job. The truth was the police had no strong desire to put these people away as most of them were known and probably locals anyway.

All information circulated and made known to us was this military operation here at Camp Gruber was to prepare and ship a complete infantry division over-seas as a unit. As we learned later this was not to be. For some reason our artillery unit did not ship out with us, neither did our commanding General nor other support groups and I never did find out why nor was any explanation given. I couldn't help wonder what were military planners thinking but the urgency for infantry replacements beckoned while other consid-erations moved to the rear. While here our days con-sisted of marching, with and without full packs, rifle range, military strategy and weapons maintenance. The military strategy one was my favorite, and a big-gie as you can tell from this story. We were supposed to be preparing to use useful tactics when engaging the enemy. Based on my later experiences, and not to be funny, our military strategy was also left stateside. Training continued into late summer and then early fall when rumors started that we would soon be on the move. Military troop movements generally were kept quiet and supposed to even be secret. I often felt this information was actually released on purpose, told in confidence, but knowing full well word would spread minimizing the impact.

Our Infantry Division was organized into three combat regiments; The 222nd, 232nd and 242nd with me being assigned to Company "L" of the 232nd. It seemed funny at the time that the term "combat" was used but I suppose that's where we would be sent. Getting used to that fact was difficult but I had to let it sink in as very real. One must remember we were very young civilians off the street and never shot at before. More correctly, "raw and green" would be more appropriate but I guess it was war and this was the way things were to be done. With the draft in place most soldier candidates would fall in this age group. The war required more infantry to the front and all news pointed toward Europe. It was clear the military was taking all replacements they could get their hands on and assignment to the infantry was what higher ups had to do. This drive to bolster the infantry was so far reaching soldiers were pulled from flight training, Officer Training School, engineer battalions, medical groups and any other operations where manpower was available. It didn't seem to matter where you were or what you were doing the replacement supply line was being prepared. Knowing that we were being lined up to fill casualty gaps was, again, not very comforting.

In later life I wondered why would the military want a complete "raw" division of civilian recruits? One would think wouldn't it have been a smarter move to send the new guys to an existing line unit to blend in with soldiers of some experience? But then, what do I know? Military planning is left up to the experts??? Rumors on moving out kept up and towards the middle of November we started to collect and organize our gear in preparation. The gear in question was merely our clothing and toiletries; weapons we didn't have and, I'm sure, would be handed out later.

7

TROOP TRAIN TO CAMP KILMER

When the word spread about leaving It appeared none of the three regiments would be allowed to visit home so as to prevent the possibility of telling where we were or of any movements. We were collectively trucked to a railroad siding loaded onto a troop train (adapted for military use) and headed out without knowing the destination (standard procedure). The trip took about three maybe four days making several stops, much of this in darkness, I guess, not to publicly announce troop movements. Stops were never long enough to get off but I don't think we were allowed anyway for fear of someone calling home so we all had to stay put. Train conditions were crowded and sleeping was done sitting up in your seat. No frills were certainly provided nor expected. Eating on board was even more difficult as we went through crowded lines to the kitchen car, get your food then work your way back to the seat juggling things on your lap. Hot food being served, cooled off quickly by the time you got back to the seat but something we just got used to.

Toilet space was also at a premium as you can imagine as lines were always there. These lines usually took up a good portion of the day. Remainder of the time we socialized and conjured up thoughts of the adventure awaiting us. No provisions for washing, except for hands, was on board so any showering would have to wait till our next camp stop. We left Camp Gruber, I think, on November 14 or 15 and arrived at our next stop Camp Kilmer, in New Jersey November 17, 1944. We were to be here for about eight days to two weeks so we were told.

This camp was a processing center only, not a training camp, where everyone here was being prepared for shipment. It was here we were issued additional clothing, weapons , blankets, helmet, heavy overcoat, and whatever else was required to travel with us overseas. Being assigned to a rifle platoon meant I now had to carry my own rifle everywhere. There was not much doubt at this stage we were headed to a devastated, bloody, war weary and cold Europe.

Where we were in New Jersey was not far from New York City so groups of us were allowed 12 hour passes on a rotating basis. All of us were cautioned not to call home. Some of us went to see a show (couldn't remember the name) but money being in short supply we also visited a local USO center to see what we could get without paying. As we learned, the military was not the best at paying on time and I felt the pinch like many others. For most of us this was our first time here so to see as much as possible the day was frantic to stretch our 12 hours as best we could. In areas like Brooklyn and the Bowery there were many bars and taverns we stopped in. Quite often the locals would buy rounds of drinks realizing our pay was really low and given our location most likely knew we were to be shipped out. Civilian beer was stronger than what we were allowed on base so it didn't take long to start talking funny. You can't see much of New York in 12 hours but we did a pretty good job. There must have been about seven in our group and just about everyone had their share of drink but no one got so bad so as to fall down. Stretching our time to the limit, we made it back on time and in one piece.

Getting around the city it made sense to ride the subway for its low cost. Even though we didn't know our way, signs were adequate and the civilians were always glad to help. Word got around from others they were approached by some character and made a pitch to make use of his "B" girls, better known as hookers. That must have sounded real good to these lonely and horny GIs but the practicality of their situation was not much time and little money. At the time we were told this they admitted not much time was spent thinking about it too long that maybe he was offering us some "freebies" but they doubted it. Somehow getting freebies for the war effort sounded patriotic but not really what this character had in mind. All of us remembered these were the kind of things to be avoided shown in training films. Causes and effects of venereal diseases would not quickly be forgotten. Nonetheless the group decided to pass on it so we will never know if that's what the offer was.

Outside of that one time pass, we were confined to camp where we would just hang out and attend some required classes relating to what was ahead. We were not allowed to call home as a security precaution. It was quite common to see all around us pictures and slogans to keep anything related to the war effort quiet because no matter what we knew the enemy was supposedly always listening, real or imagined. This business of not talking about anything war related was, however, taken seriously. One of the most famous slogans was," loose lips can sink ships". Later when we got to see Germany they were doing the same kinds of things on posters scattered about on buildings.

Trying as we did to have a good time and show a happy face it was hard to cover our emotions and feelings. The raw truth we all knew was we were there for one reason; to ship out and become part of the war. There was nothing we could do to change things so we tried hard to show acceptance of whatever fate was to come our way and to do the best we could. During this time we gave thought to see if we wanted to make changes to the beneficiaries of our service life insurance. Uncle Sam must have thought we had high value for the insurance was for $10,000, a tidy sum then. Most of us did just that, for it was folly to think we would all make it back. For me I didn't have many options to think about so my remaining family at home was my choice.

Many of us also took time to write home and give words of encouragement to our families. We had to be careful with our words for it was banned to describe our location and purpose. All this we had been previously lectured too so it was a bit difficult to exchange anything meaningful. Wartime mail was always censored and the originating location postmark was not allowed to be shown.

8

THE PERILOUS OCEAN CROSSING

Our time here was about one week, shorter than we were told. This again may have been an indicator of the serious manpower problem. Under cover of darkness we loaded onto trucks and brought to a rail yard. From here we traveled to the port of debarkation by train then unloaded by regiment and marched to the docks where we had to reassemble. Typical of the military, a protocol had to be followed to check those present and to be accounted for. In due time orders came to board by regiment beginning the long process. Loading about two thousand plus troops up the gangway carrying their equipment used up many hours. Once on board the crew guided us to our space way below in the bowels of the ship. Our ship was one of the mass produced " Liberty" ships. Along the loading area ship names such as; "Bienville", "Taylor" and "Alexander" were mentioned but I don't remember which one I was boarding (they looked like they were not built too good anyway). During the voyage I found out I was on the "Bienville". Each of us was assigned a bunk of very limited space for ourselves, duffel bag, rifle, helmet and all other gear as well. This loading took place on November 24 and was to be my home for the next 14 days.

We sailed early the next morning. I seem to remember none of the troops were supposed to be on deck as we sailed out of the harbor but many of us worked our way up anyway. Not much effort was made to get us below. Others below decks took turns and got a glimpse of the Statue of Liberty through portholes. As we started our trip none of us knew our destination (not that we were supposed to know) nor did it matter to most of us for we knew we would be shot at soon enough. My humble living quarters was not for the squeamish for I was at or below the water line and near the outer hull. Several days out of port the ocean started to become angry and unruly causing the ship to start a rolling and heaving motion, For those that never sailed on a poorly built ship this motion causes some very noticeable noises as the metal twists by the ship's movements. This same motion also started the parade of hundreds of GI's to the rail or head (as the bathroom was called) and wherever else they could find for the unpleasantness of sea sickness. The head and many parts of the ship received a lot of action especially in the first 3 to 5 days.

There are not too many ways to describe the sight of hundreds of us GI's vomiting on an open deck in windy conditions. The sight of this is as gross as it sounds for vomit was literally flying in all directions. For those not sickened going out on deck at this time required bravery so staying below made sense. The crew and many of us were assigned the task of washing down the ship constantly and cleaning up this man made mess as best we could. The mess hall (military for where to eat) was way below decks and where cooking odors further irritated our queasy stomachs. For most of us things got considerably better on about the 4th or 5th day as we adjusted to the ships motion.

How did we know our trip was for 14 days? It was easy. When boarding ship each of us was handed a mess card with space for 28 punches and we were told earlier there would be two meals per day. This, we were told, was a method to control food consumption for planning purposes. What they didn't tell us was with several thousand of us eating, the long lines would take up a good part of the day anyway. Even so, we still had time to spare because spending time below in our bunks proved to be pretty uncomfortable and was minimized. Many meals would not be taken simply because of the constant vomiting during the first few days. On board we could purchase some items like apples, cigarettes, and candy bars from the ships store (similar to the PX) at modest prices.

Life at sea was not always our own. Regimental commanders somehow made arrangements to have work assignments for each of their groups. This was okay as a way to give us something to do rather than just sitting around. One group would work below decks, another would do guard duty and one for above deck clean up and policing. To add some fairness the work was rotated every three or four days to even things out. Beyond this, we kept up on maintaining our rifles clean, lubricated and practicing assembly and disassembly. Although we were assigned things to do a good portion of the day was spent getting fed. Our own time included writing mail that would be delivered back to the states from the next stop. Gambling in the form of shooting craps and playing poker could be found throughout the ship. The big problem was finding suitable space.

Throughout the trip we had to respond to drills when alarms were sounded. Officers constantly drummed into us the importance of this and everyone took these very seriously and did everything expected of us. None of us had to be reminded we were in the Atlantic, a major supply route, and Germany's U-Boats had been devastating Allied shipping. In our bunks at night we talked about getting torpedoed and what our chances would be. Given our location near the water line would make the ending rather quick. Being jammed in as we were we realistically could not move anywhere in a hurry so the water would get us. We have all seen how ships are built with those big bulkheads. Within these are openings called hatches and not very big at that. In an emergency there would be no way hundreds of GI's could ever get through to a way topside. For those that might be lucky enough to get out the thoughts of jumping in the cold water was not very welcome. Estimates of survivability in the frigid northern waters ranged anywhere from twenty minutes to maybe two hours. Our vulnerability was obvious and extremely sobering. Newsreels shown in the theaters were a constant reminder of ships being sunk. A troop ship like ours are the ones with a big bulls eye target on the side and would be a particularly tempting prize for the enemy below.

To dramatize the danger the following information is from the public records and actually happened in the same month of our crossing. A former Belgian luxury liner designed to carry only several hundred people was converted for troop transport and renamed " Leopoldville". This ship was carrying over 2,200 American soldiers from England to France. Off the coast of Cherbourg, France it was torpedoed on December 24th

(Christmas Eve) 1944 by the U- 486. This area near the English Channel always had rough water conditions which seriously hampered rescue operations. Nearby English warships tried under difficult conditions to save as many as possible knowing enemy subs were still in the area. The horror and chaos of survival continued until the ship went under. Searching for those in the water presented many obstacles. Rough seas prevented many from being seen and caused them to drift some distance from the main area of rescue. When the accounting of this tragedy was tallied and put into hard numbers, 763 soldiers were declared to be lost. Sad to say these soldiers died before firing a shot. They, like us, were sorely needed to replace the mounting ground casualties. Those poor souls were crammed into very tight spaces much as we were with little to no chance to save themselves. This terrible news was withheld from the public for a long time.

After we were at sea a couple of days, from seemingly out of nowhere, other ships joined us until we formed quite a large convoy and as we looked around there appeared to be a good size naval presence to provide escort. If these words sound vague it's because of the difficulty to observe at sea particularly without binoculars. I never did find out how many ships there were in total (I suppose we weren't supposed to know anyway) but it was a normal curiosity.

Troop ships and other transports were kept in a steady formation and speed controlled. Our escorts, the navy destroyers, capable of moving quicker attempted to shield us from attackers by sweeping the outer flanks. From deck we could not see far enough in the distance because weather was a factor as well. Unless you lived in a cave It didn't take much intelligence to figure that the enemy was out looking for targets like ours and could be lurking about not far away. I'm sure that kind of thinking was on every ones mind, imagined or real. Shipping losses were made public in the newspapers, on the radio and in newsreels shown in theaters. Whether the Government showed true losses can only be a matter of conjecture. There was a belief at home and now in the service that news reports were " doctored" or withheld altogether.

Our transport ship was part of the armed merchant fleet which meant it was staffed by civilians but had navy personnel to man the guns who periodically did test firings. Navy gunners derived some pleasure to do practice firings unannounced and when not expected just to rattle our nerves. This firing was quite noisy in the decks just below but could be felt most anywhere on the ship.

Activities gradually reduced to writing letters, playing poker, guard duty, talking to your buddies and eating. Eating was a slow process due to the sheer numbers aboard and most likely the real reason why they served only two meals. Even these two meals must have been a real challenge for the kitchen. We were summoned by groups and when that happened long lines had to form, pass through several small passageways leading to the mess hall. Food served, I guess, was typical navy chow, not the best but filling. I was not fussy about food and with only two meals per day I had no problem finishing what I had in front of me. The system allowed as the saying goes; " only one bite of the apple" meaning a single pass through the line. Mess hall space was restrictive to the extent everyone at the tables had to stand up for no stools were provided anyway. This standing only was a method to move things along and seemed to work. Tables were long and narrow and had a lip all around so trays would not slide off as the ship rolled. If motion was bad enough there would be spills anyway. As mentioned earlier, the assigned meal cards were punched for each time through the line allowing each soldier 28 meals. For most of us though, we never did get all the meals because for the first three or four days eating took a back seat to unruly seasickness with its accompanying unpleasantness.

After several days at sea we were allowed to spend time on deck both day and night. While there we did exercises as a group to maintain some level of readiness. When on deck at night there could be no light for any reason. Even smoking (very popular in those days) could not be done on an open deck. Ships deck doors were rigged to put lights out when opened, a pretty standard feature for all wartime vessels and voyages. On the open deck required dressing warmly as the night temperatures were quite cool and winds whipped harshly and steadily.

Shipboard showers, navy style, are a real experience as well as being contained in a cramped space. Time was allotted for each group and carefully rationed because of the volume of people and the amount of hot water made aboard ship. Showering was done in salt water and we were given soap made for that purpose but it was still difficult, and darn near impossible to generate a lather. Certainly not the best of conditions but at least the water was hot, our skin felt sticky when finished, but better than nothing.

Our convoy seemed to be following a more northerly route and the ocean showed it becoming increasingly rough. Word spread we would go through part of the North Sea and bring much more discomfort. I never did find out if we were actually in the North Sea but it did get really rough with huge waves. I'm no expert on the sea but our ship was tossing heavily.

My assigned quarters way below decks and close to the outer hull gave off loud noises and banging as the ship would rise and fall back. To get a clearer picture of this we would try to go on deck during daytime and watch other ships in the distance (those that we could see) moving about in the same heavy seas. Being on deck under these conditions was discouraged as being dangerous so we kept the time above short. Any time on deck would expose one to getting quite wet anyway. Below decks was the place to be, still quite uncomfortable but out of the weather.

This scene was scary to say the least. Watching other transports like ours we could see the bow come way out of the water then come crashing down making them shake and vibrate. Then the other half of the ship would rise out of the water where we could see their propellers (screws) rotating in the air. I often wondered, if the deck guns had to be fired how on earth could they be manned or even aimed effectively? I should have asked one of the gun crew but never did. This type weather must have suited U-boats for they could operate submerged. Our forward speed wasn't very much but had to be tied in to the convoy's coordinated plan. This motion continued for about three days before smoothing out which finally gave way to making our existence more bearable. In weather like this having to stay below on our crowded ship limited our movements and added to the discomfort.

Liberty Ships like the one we were on didn't have a very good reputation in the early days of the war. Being made in volume meant quantity over quality. It was known that early versions had structural problems and some did break up in harsh ocean conditions. Again, not a comforting thought. Disastrous events and other wartime blunders were usually kept from the press and the public and not divulged until many years later. In fact some blunders or other screw-ups causing large troop losses were not revealed until maybe 40 years after the war ended.

At some point word was we turned to a southerly direction for what seemed to be about four days resulting in a much smoother ride. From what we could see many ships of the convoy were still with us but others moved away, it seemed. With little fanfare and at night word quickly spread that we were about to pass through the strait of Gibraltar. How this was known I wasn't sure but most of us suspect it was from a crew member. Being at sea it would appear not to be any security breach. We could see lights from Morocco on our starboard side but Gibraltar to port was blacked out. None of us had any clear knowledge of the tactical situation in Europe so any thinking on destination would be speculation. What we did know was that we were an incomplete piecemeal division heading somewhere. All we could do was our daily activities and wait until docking in port. The size of our convoy now seems to be smaller than when in the North Sea but our escort presence was still with us. The Mediterranean was also a much smoother ride and on next to the very last day we found out our destination port would be Marseille in southern France.

9

MARSEILLE AND COMMAND POST 2

Our ship along with many others docked here on December 7, 1944

(exactly three years after Pearl Harbor day) but not allowed to disembark until the next day. This port, one of the largest and busiest ports in Europe, was overflowing with war time commerce. The active ground war front by now had moved many miles to the north. While all movements of men and material were done openly we still were in range of enemy aircraft from other locations. As such we were told this and be ready to take cover on short notice when sirens might sound. Before disembarking, the entire group was given a strong lecture on problems we could encounter in Marseille. This city which had a bad reputation anyway and for years has been a melting pot for many different cultures. The war only aggravated this situation with many different uniforms passing through, each with their own brand of baggage and trouble.

Our regimental commanders were particularly concerned for our health where venereal disease was prevalent. We were told Marseille had as many prostitutes as a small city perhaps drawn there to service the foreign multitudes passing through. Due to the make-up of this busy city the type of diseases were especially virulent and not easily treatable. "Hookers" were to be avoided but would be the ones most likely soliciting in bars, on the streets, and in restaurants. The large numbers of prostitutes we later found resulted from a large age spread, said to be maybe 14 to 60. Sad to see what people will do to make a living and how the years of war affected those surrounded by conflict. Our commanders also knew we were human, cooped up for a long time and knew we would be looking for some kind of " entertainment".

The military had prepared a list of "approved" houses where the females were examined periodically (some relief in that, I guess). It didn't take much intelligent thought this was a safer bet but beyond that after any encounter we were strongly encouraged to get checked out at what was called a military "pro-station". These were also part of our lecture and told there were a number of them scattered around the city. When visiting these we needed to be patient as they may be quite busy due to the good hooker business. These stations would provide for washing of our

80

private parts and application of medications as a preventative measure. This preferred military treatment became famous during the war and was known as " Blue Ointment" the then state of the art medicine for treating venereal diseases. Treatment at these pro stations and this colorful material became a humorous conversation topic for quite a while then as well as years later. As humorous as it sounded our commanders reminded us this was serious business as any venereal disease would be most unpleasant and could have long time consequences.

After disembarking, we were loaded onto open top trucks and given a ride (driven by military lunatics) through the narrow streets of Marseille that lasted longer than I cared to remember. During the ride we had to slow down and even stop several times and when we did hordes of kids would show up rather quickly. They would surround the truck and beg for cigarettes, canned goods, candy, tooth paste or anything available for that matter. It didn't take long to learn these kids would steal from you if they got too close. Part of growing up in wartime and it's desperation. These kids were also selling the services of their sisters and even their mothers for anything they could get; just another sad aspect of the consequences of war. Observing for the first time what war was all about left many distasteful lingering images. After a very uncomfortable ride for about 15 miles bumping, bouncing and turning much of the way we arrived at our next stop called Command Post 2, CP 2 for short.

This was a large tent city in a hilly area set up to prepare us to be sent somewhere labeled as a forward position to be most likely, shot at, guard duty, or whatever assignment was next. We would be here for about nine days. Reports from up north continued to exhibit confusion as to where the German strength might be sent. So based on what the commanders thought would determine our next assignment. With so many unknowns didn't seem to bode well for the next move. The first two nights it rained a lot and was cold and we didn't have enough blankets to be comfortable. Worse yet, this area had a bit of rain before we arrived so the ground was muddy and since no bunks were there meant we had to sleep on the ground. We each had a blanket and raincoat but the extra blankets we needed were in our duffel bags which trailed behind us by at least a day. Unloading the support gear from a transport ship for a couple thousand troops would take several days and was no easy task. No showers and not much else was available here. The tents offered protection from the rain but little help from the cold so conditions could be described as Spartan. Night time was really cold, damp and uncomfortable so we tried to huddle close together to generate some body warmth. This helped a bit but still not suitable for any meaningful sleep. We really needed our duffel bag with the other blankets which didn't show up for a couple of days.

It was sometimes hard to comprehend the mindset of our military leaders. Here we were being prepared for combat, supposedly as a division, but our Commanding General, Harry J. Collins along with artillery and other needed support units were still back in the states. No matter, for "grunts" like us we knew orders would come down from someone somewhere and they were. Maybe in the real world combat planning is done by officers with time up front and way below the rank of General. Hollywood's version of war movies rarely showed confusion or lack of leadership because their wars were always well organized, orderly and followed the script and the director.

Our time here was primarily one of waiting while the commanders decided where to send us. All of the clothing and our weapons were already in our possession. Rifle platoons such as I was in only had rifles and were expected to be carried. Other platoons with what was called heavy weapons couldn't be easily carried and required trucks to move around. So to keep us occupied we were allowed to move about the area. Time off was given so groups of us headed into town but again lectured before leaving to stay away from the "street walkers" and any other groups of foreigners. The only means to travel was by army trucks so we did our best to hook rides on whatever was moving in that direction. Since supplies were constantly being shuffled to our campsite, trucks moved back and forth from the port area steadily. Some others in the camp that had already experienced Marseille suggested we take along cigarettes, can goods, shaving supplies and anything that could used for bartering, primarily for drinks. Experience from those before us even suggested those items could go farther than U.S. dollars or wartime currency. For those so inclined, bartering would include the women as well but, as advised, to be avoided. Others took butter, bacon, sugar and salt but no matter what you had everything was very popular in the bars and throughout the city. Getting these food items was no easy task. The only way was to make friends with the kitchen crew and use money and cigarettes and maybe beg a little. If there was something needed you could usually get what was wanted for a price.

Everything in the city was in short supply so we did well getting our share of drinks, perhaps too many. Drinking in these smelly bars turned out to be an adventure for they were quite dirty and unappealing. For one thing, what was on the shelves were bottles not known to many of us. So we took turns sampling to see what might be agreeable but choices were difficult. There was great concern for cleanliness especially the drinking glasses. In these places they spent little time washing glasses and hot soapy water was not readily seen. After a short while most of us narrowed our choices to brandy(here it's cognac) and lousy beer cooled by placing it outside. Refrigeration and any ice making, a real luxury in wartime, was in short supply. Most things available in wartime had questionable quality anyway. Still it was enough to get us in a good mood without passing out but some of us came close.

We all had our share of drinks so when it came time to use the bathroom this opened up a whole new experience, strange to us but quite normal in 1944 Europe. Bathrooms in the drinking places were usually in a small basement room and consisted of a hole in the floor with foot imprints to help align you. More noticeable there was no gender distinction, with one size fits all. This hole in the floor was out in the open with no effort to enclose it like a stall. One of our friends had just barely zipped up when without any concern a young woman after waiting came in, positioned herself over the hole, squatted and relieved herself. Things like this showed cultural differences between Europeans and ourselves where they have less hang-ups. Maybe it isn't fair to paint all with the same brush but rather to blame the long years of war for the apathy and apparent lack of modesty. Terrible living conditions and war experiences surely made their lives and attitudes hardened. We are fortunate in America for not having to go through any of that.

There are not many ways to describe wartime Marseille other than to call it a hellhole. Even better, it could easily be the armpit of southern France. Everything was rundown, had wide areas of war damage and generally pretty dirty. With a war on not many people were concerned about how the place looked; survival was the primary concern. Along many streets were sidewalk stalls, not very big, where men and even some women would urinate into the gutter. Not very pretty or sanitary but then a fact of life. This city being a large shipping center brought sailors from many countries where after some drinking in the bars it wouldn't take much to start a fight. We were correctly told these sailors most always carried knives so, as advised, we traveled in groups for protection. This was good advice that we followed and seemed to work. One thing we counted on extensively was to travel in areas patrolled by the Military Police (MP). The MP's, as their name implies are cops in military uniform whose job it was to protect America's GI's from others as well as from themselves.

Our group traveling around the city consisted of seven of us. Myself and several others just turned eighteen but as you would expect one of the older ones took it on himself to become leader. This leader convinced enough of the others to become men by going to one of those " houses. " He had taken the trouble to find the location of several in areas close by. There was not much reason to fight it at the time so we all went along. So my next wild experience was a trip to the military approved whorehouse (probably bordello in French). Calling it a whorehouse gave it more stature than what we usually referred to as a "Cathouse". We were all young and most likely not married. Some members of our group would tease the youngest about getting laid suggesting we might not make it home and should go for it just in case. If for some reason you were uncomfortable with this and tried to back out you would be called sissies, fags, mama's boys or worse. The torment from your buddies we knew would continue with little letup so that backing out was not a realistic option. It made sense to get in line, get laid and eliminate any future harassment. This legal business establishment (?) was in a typical row house set into street blocks and I'm sure was some ones home before this. These " houses" were on several levels like a townhouse with stairs lined with hordes of GI's and soldiers and sailors from other countries awaiting their turn. At the lower level, shop owners would take your money and place you in a line and told to just follow along after the others in front (I don't remember what it cost in war time francs).This scene would be similar to going to a carnival and getting in line for the Ferris Wheel.

Actually it was a bit comical being a production like assembly line operation. It was, after all, quite a large business and seemingly thriving. When you got to the top of the stairs, available "house ladies" of a wide variety of ages, sizes and shapes, and dressed for business would try to grab you quickly. I'm sure they were paid by the quantity of customers processed (I didn't want to call it piece work). I wondered if the authorities set age limits for this kind of occupation? These professionals also knew all of us had not been with a woman in quite a while so it wouldn't take long for us to finish the encounter. It was a shop require-ment, rightfully so, to use condoms and these gals were experts in helping us put them on properly and making sure we did our business in a timely fashion. Doing this maybe thirty times a day would hone the necessary skills. For them, time was money. Com-pared to other jobs I'm fairly sure they made a decent income but in a terribly bad occupation.

During our stay here I and others went to Mar-seille three times mostly to see the sights such as they were. At least we learned what drinks to order and what to watch out for. Before leaving camp we could find out the areas with a higher presence of MP's and guided ourselves accordingly. Back in CP2 when gathered in groups we talked openly about experiences in the city and how to best describe Marseille. One of the best I thought was this statement; "If it became necessary to give France an encma, Marseille would be where you would put the plug". There was little doubt from all, this was a most undesirable place, war damaged, dirty and wouldn't be missed. Our sympathies remained with the poor bastards who had to live through this and still call it home.

The reality that we were now near or in a war zone came to us when a siren sounded and anti-aircraft fire started. It seems that German planes most likely from Italy came over the area where later we were told was a scouting mission to keep an eye on allied shipping and military operations. Shrapnel from this shooting of thousands of rounds became a hazard for much of it fell over the entire camp. I don't know how many people know that spent ordinance just falling from altitude can be very dangerous and even fatal. Because we had been advised earlier about this we sought cover but being in tents didn't help us much but that's all we had. It wasn't long before the planes made their pass and moved away. Flights like this, we were told, were done periodically for intelligence gathering and to show they could still do it. Still, it was an introduction for the noisy and exciting things sure to come.

10

UP FRONT TO THE ORDEAL

From here in CP2 we were taken by trucks to a railroad siding and loaded into boxcars on or about December 19 on the narrow gauge railroad quite common in Europe and headed north. We wondered about the wisdom of transporting us this way. Trains were always a tempting target and these had holes in them to prove that point. I'm also sure a column of trucks would be an equally good target. These cars seemed to resemble the famous " 40&8" cars many elders might remember from that earlier world war. These relic box cars were labeled, in French, on their sides to carry 40 men or 8 horses. For some reason we thought we were to be assigned to General Patton's 3rd Army based on scuttlebutt/rumor, etc., but, later found out were to be rerouted to the 7th Army at Strasbourg to bolster troop count. It was this area that little action was expected and routine patrolling to be in order. Further north near Belgium planners felt would be the location of a strong German counter-offensive.

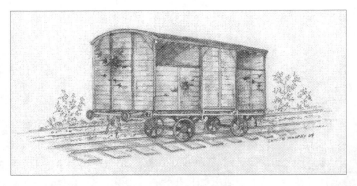

40 & 8 BOX CAR

As we traveled, the only way we could see the passing country around us was to look through the many openings in the sides and doors. These openings I refer to were not designed in but as a result of damage from getting shot up by enemy planes. Our travel carried us north and west of Strasburg initially but then easterly and closer to the front. This change in routing brought us close enough to Metz where artillery was heard some distance away then to another town whose name I can't recall. After unloading, from here we formed a long convoy and traveled in open trucks to Strasbourg arriving on the afternoon of the 22nd. Here we spent the night in a large building that appeared to be a school or university of some sort.

The area north and east of Strasbourg was also known as "Alsace-Lorraine". We didn't know much about its history, nor were we told, but it seems a large section of this area was for a long time under German rule and because of the wars fought in this area lines were redrawn as part of surrender terms. While officially part of France now, Germany had long claimed or sought to annex this region. Our commanders for some reason didn't think it was important to let us know this. It was quite a surprise to us then as we moved about this area German was the primary spoken language. Being part of France the residents also spoke French but it was said many of them joined and fought for Germany as that was apparently where their allegiance was. Look at some of these not so French names of towns in France; Bitche, Rittershoffen, Strasbourg, Gambsheim, Kilstett, and many others. Also not surprising , we were told, was that we should be careful about army talk when moving among the civilians around us. The Rhine was a little distance to the east and what separated us fro m the Germans. For the next three or four days we moved around to close by villages but never too far from Strasbourg. On the outskirts here we spent Christmas by going to church where the mass was given in Latin (as expected for that time) but the sermon was in both French and German,......strange? There was little joy for this holiday as the general mood was somber but some humor was attempted to break the chill. We were not being shot at for the moment but one look around the area spoke for itself. Things could change very quickly as we were now certainly within artillery and aircraft range.

The next day our company was loaded onto trucks and taken to a Fort Fransecky some distance away and from there moved again out into the countryside near a town called Gambsheim (I'm wasn't sure about the name in the beginning but for the events to happen later would become forever entrenched in my mind). Some of us were billeted in private homes and a room was assigned for viewing the surrounding area. Just about every house around showed some kind of damage. People that lived here were afraid and for good reason. This area has a long history of war. Germans had occupied this town before, leaving scars on these unfortunate people. Needless to say, the truly French people had a lot more to worry about than those Germanic. For the next few hours the trucks would take small groups of our company and place us along remote areas where there would only be dirt roads maybe a few houses and not much else. Movements we went through for the past couple of days were to say the least, confusing. These places we were brought to might be called a village or hamlet but it didn't matter much and who cared.

What did matter was we were now not too far from the Rhine with a lot of experienced well armed

Germans on their side and then told things could expect to heat up at any time which sounded like a contradiction to words passing around. The trucks left and we had barely gotten into our defensive positions when some shooting started to come our way and being " new recruits " confusion was present. Using the term defensive position means that when you are getting shot at you learn very quickly to seek cover. Near buildings you get inside, if outside you fall to the ground and find what's available. We had a real problem for the ones shooting at us could not be seen easily. Around the houses were clearings but not too far away there were stands of closely spaced trees which provided them good cover. Some of us were in a position to return fire but selecting a suitable target proved difficult. It was widely believed no Germans were supposed to be on our side of the Rhine in this area but events quickly proved otherwise. Getting shot at quickly dispels those rumors. The shooting didn't last very long and then they moved away quickly obscured by the thick tree cover. We were not ordered to seek them out nor in a position to do them much harm either. Getting information from our officers or their non-coms scooting around in jeeps was sketchy at best. A realistic picture of what was going on was not available. Their wasn't much we could do except to see if any orders were coming down. Being where we were I wondered if this scouting information got back to a place called headquarters, wherever that was.

This was our first encounter and not knowing much more we concluded it was just a small patrol gathering information. We had no experience in combat and just assumed things but now knew somehow Germans had moved to our side of the Rhine. Patrols like that, we guessed, would only have small arms to move about quietly and quickly. After a while, myself and the others didn't know who or what to believe. I need to point out when our two squads were dropped off and spread out in small groups having only small arms we were ill prepared to do much harm to those shooting at us anyway. Infantry like us usually dig holes in the ground for protection but it was very cold and digging could not be done. The best we could do for cover was to make use of the houses, barns and the board fences between them and little else. It shouldn't take too much imagination to know what protection a house or a wooden fence represents against machine guns and the 88 mm's on their tanks. This we would learn a little later the hard way.

The next day In the distance against a snowy and cold background Germans could be seen again stretched out for a distance but in the beginning it looked like just another, maybe a little larger patrol.

The question we kept wondering was, how could this happen again without us being told? Since they were still some distance away many of us moved back into the houses and to the upper floors from orders by the non com. Other GI's around us were told to take suitable cover and be prepared for any move they might make. There was a lot of movement in their direction but it looked as if they just wanted to rattle us but would not move in at this time. From information passed down there was still no indication they crossed the river and were now on our side but here they were again. It was early morning when the shooting started and by now our company knew we were under attack. Other sections of our platoon found out by radio that this activity was going on over a large section of the Rhine. We were not big in size, far from it, but being spread out in the fields and houses might have forced them to assess the attack strategy. We weren't in any position to seriously threaten them but how could they know that?

Being isolated from our supply base our ammunition had to be conserved so we shot back when we had a reasonable target. When and how to shoot is something we would have to learn. Because of distance we couldn't tell if any damage had been done during that short exchange then for some reason they slipped away again out of our sight. Throughout the exchange

I don't think they got any closer than about 700 yards but these people were well versed and showed it. It appeared to us that they had no intentions of a heavy engagement at this time and were simply scouting again. Later we found out many other patrols were being sent out over a wide section along the Rhine presumably to spot areas of weakness. This large section was covered by our three Infantry Regiments, all of us untested and without artillery besides. My particular platoon had only rifles. These patrols were a prelude to a much larger attack that was to happen soon but not known to us then.

Shortly after this, some sections of our platoon were pulled back and summoned to a small town outside of Strasbourg. A plan was being put together for a small group to attack a section of the "Siegfried Line" in our area which would have required crossing the Rhine in rubber boats in darkness. The purpose, we were told, was to see if we could take some Germans as prisoners for later questioning. Somehow lost in all this was some of our commanders towards the rear were out of touch. They were talking about crossing the Rhine to get some Germans but we knew they were already on our side of the river, at least when they wanted to. It was hard for us to understand why the planners didn't know all that we knew. It would seem they moved freely across the river when it was required and without being noticed. Still no reason for those "upstairs" not to know of these events. A raid like this would have required it to be done quickly and quietly. For reasons we never found out the plan was scrapped. This plan, to me, was ill advised and would have been a disaster anyway. Remember, we are talking about raw recruits of the first order with no combat experience and being shot at for the first time. It would be laughable to think of this as a well planned operation.

From that thinking, and our later experiences, it was my belief we didn't have anyone capable of making plans for a covert operation of this type. Here we were a very green infantry regiment with no combat experience. What were they thinking? I would like to think the insanity of this became apparent to someone and, ultimately, ditched the whole idea. Without question our troops including myself would have been wiped out because these same sections of the German lines were actually being built up to division strength levels for a major offensive to be called "Nordwind" and to take place in just the next few days! How was it that this buildup was not known to our commanders? Once again we returned by truck to our former positions. It might have been some kind of an omen, for the next few days we would once again encounter patrols with their small arms fire. It appeared the

Germans might be testing us. This type shooting was exchanged again periodically as we were moved around the area in many of the nearby villages and maybe to prime us for things to come. Perhaps the Germans were playing games and toying with us but to us it was not obvious and getting shot at any time is serious business. These places tended to look quite similar so when we moved around it looked like we were actually in the same place. I Don't know what these movements were accomplishing, maybe it was a strategy (hard to believe), but we hoped the enemy was getting as confused as we were. We were to learn very shortly the Germans were not confused at all and deadly serious about their next move. As all this was being done I couldn't help but wonder was this business of constantly making troop movements something being done by other divisions in the war zone? To think this might be a strategy used in all locations gnawed away at me for some time. I never did find an answer to this.

From the days before Christmas of 1944 until New Years our activities consisted of much of the same. Slowed down by snow we again were shuffled to other nearby villages, sometimes for two days at a time then moved back. The Germans continued to send patrols where and when of their choosing and we offered whatever small resistance we could muster.

This was not a Christmas most of us envisioned but here we were. Hot food was a rarity for no field mess hall was nearby and any semblance of hot food could only get to us by truck. It was usually cold by the time we got to it as bitter winter weather was all around us. In our situation we were probably considered lucky to get rations dropped off at all for the consistent patrols we encountered. American trucks moving around so close to the front would draw the enemy's attention and become risky. Anything on our side that moved would be considered fair game anyway.

Between Christmas and New Years heavy snows fell over the area followed by real low temperatures. For a short while we all hunkered down, things got real quiet and in some sense the war seemed to stop. Then in the early days of January , 2nd., 3rd.and 4th of 1945 and depending on where some action was we were once again moved around in several small villages; Sessenheim, Illsburg, Gambsheim and Killstett. All of this area within 20 kilometers of Strasbourg was to become a political hot bed due to major wrangling at the highest levels of the Allied Command. If you can find a better word for organized confusion it would have been spread around here but by now we were getting quite used to it. We would be put on trucks and taken somewhere, then the next day be asked to assemble for a march. Then, without much notice, told to get ready to move out and once again put onto trucks and moved back to where we were. This widely disputed conduct at the highest levels was summarily written up in the January 1995 issue of the VFW magazine[*].

At issue, was that Generals Dwight Eisenhower and Jacob Devers felt they should withdraw to a more defensible position in the foothills of the Low Vosges Mountain. To do this would mean the city of Strasbourg would be abandoned by defense forces which then could be overrun by the Germans with little resistance. This didn't sit well with French General Charles de Gaulle and he threatened to defend the city alone. Strasbourg was a symbol of French rule (and pride) in an area formerly annexed from Germany and from the French perspective could not be abandoned. As it turned out, Eisenhower relented and plans were made to defend Strasbourg and the surrounding area.

These decisions by the higher ups may have been the reason why our regiments were scattered so thin and very vulnerable. Our Division the 42nd infantry was part of the Seventh Army under the command of General Alexander Patch. Some distance north of us a very major battle was beginning to form in an area of Belgium that would be remembered historically as the "Battle of the bulge". Military planners must have shared the belief that the operation there was far more important to defend than other areas of the front to the south where we were. As a consequence General Patton's Third Army was directed to send some of his divisions north to provide support for the "Bulge" defense. These moves directly resulted in elements of Patch's Seventh Army, most notably our orphan regiments, to be spread out even more in an attempt to fill the voids left in this line. Description of this move included; "..........leaving this sector perilously thin" *.

During the war years with its reporting in the newspapers and newsreels, Generals and their commands were seem to be given a level of prominence. Whether deserved or not the media of the day gave these men what would be akin to hero status. Before I went into the service I also felt these Commanders should be held in high esteem for their service. But I must tell you, after what I went through I had a problem with respect for them. Maybe my beliefs were unfair, but looking up to them in later life was a bit beyond my reach.

This latest movement to the north caused the remaining armies (which included myself and many other recruits) to be spread out extremely thin. From the city of Saarbrucken in the north and following the Rhine south to below Strasbourg for about 125 miles became known as the "Lauterbourg Bulge" *. With all of this attention on the "Big Bulge" to the north

German planners apparently saw a weakness in our area to the south and prepared for a strong move to regain lost ground. Further, it might have been Hitler's statement that Germany was intact and a force still to be reckoned with. This American military weakness was written up in the same VFW magazine with statements like;" The 232nd infantry regiment manned 33 miles of front" [*], presenting an unreasonable and dangerous situation. We were about to have our own unrecognized "Smaller Battle of the Bulge" but without the means for any realistic resistance. What we were about to go through did not become headline news and received little notice. Worse yet, we later learned as things got progressively threatening we would be on our own and to expect no help.

---

[*] *Excerpts reprinted by permission of the VFW Magazine, January,1995 & March, 1995.*

11

RESISTANCE AND THEN CAPTURE

About January 2nd or 3rd, ,1945 two platoons of our Company "L" were, once again, driven to a small hamlet, probably near or on the outskirts of Gambsheim. Our other two platoons one with our heavy weapons were moved to Killstett several kilometers away. After awhile and with all our movements all villages, as said before, started to look alike. The continual movements were now way beyond getting us confused. We were dropped off with only what we could carry, food and ammunition, and as the trucks were leaving stated that our commanders ordered us to; "HOLD AT ALL COSTS" !!!! What the hell was this? Did they at this time know more than we were being told? Were they telling us to expect very bad things and nothing could be done about it? Were they telling us to do the best we could but expect the worst? That statement resonated in our ears, didn't give us much comfort, and sounded like our death knell which for many it was soon to be.

Once the trucks left we were on our own with no further contact with company headquarters except by radio which only our lieutenant had. Spread out as we were there was little individual contact with him. Most of us thought that statement was still a little strange for we were continually led to believe we would encounter only small patrols in this sector with the big action much further North, the big "Bulge". The planning was, as usual, great. Who knows, maybe our regimental commanders were also frustrated, confused, following their orders and didn't know any more than we did. For the moment, our platoon still had this one jeep to contact those in this sector. Lt. Buck drove around and had to appraise the situation quickly and give us his orders. Given these orders our squads spread out and sought suitable positions. Most of us moved into houses not only for better viewing but to get out of the cold. Others moved to the pill boxes located near the village but was more distant from us than desired. These pill boxes were much closer to the Rhine and would take the first hit of any assault. Some took up positions near the barns where large bales of hay were available. For the moment our jeep kept circulating around the area as we then went into a waiting mode. All of us were advised to be vigilant and to observe for enemy movements. Being outside was not pleasant. It was quite cold and snow was about knee deep and the evening sky showed signs more could be on the way.

As stated earlier, and to emphasize our peril, our platoons were "rifle platoons". The "heavy weapons platoons", something we could have really used, were about five kilometers away in Killstett with other elements of our regiment and of no use to us. Coupled with that as mentioned, our artillery tanks and Commanding General were still in the states or on the high seas somewhere, go figure!!!!! The orders of "HOLD AT ALL COSTS" was to become the title of a book published by the 42nd Rainbow Division Veterans Memorial Foundation. Somewhere around 1988 an effort began to collect the personal accounts of POWs. For some reason I never found out about this literary effort or how it was handled so my story was not included in that book. Not getting My Story in that publication was a strong incentive to producing this book. Later, the decision was made to publish the stories and reached the public in 2004.Why this work was done some 50 years after the fact is any ones guess. What this book did accomplish was to give uncensored personal accounts of military confusion and the resulting human ordeal. The book delves into uncharted accounts of the seemingly absence of organized planning. This resulted in the placement of green recruits into a vulnerable and no win situation.

This descriptive accounting in their own words are personal stories from the many POW's of how our regiments were placed into near impossible combat conditions. It clearly demonstrates how those orders resulted in the high losses and the number of prisoners. From those accounts how the so called "Geneva Convention" failed in so many ways or never existed at all. These personal accounts will again support the unflattering comments of how our short and devastating war was conducted. If our commanders knew a major attack was coming in our area and allowed only rifle platoons to defend our sector says very little for their competence. Those of us lucky enough to survive, in fairness, might say our commanders were only following orders, told to deal with it and powerless to change things. Soldiers are supposed to follow orders and not question their superiors. I, and the others, intended to do that but thought it would be nice to have a reasonable chance of success. It was not to be, so like in poker you have to work with the hand you are dealt. Indeed, it seemed we were cannon fodder, assigned a task, and subsequently overwhelmed by the enemy. It would be said this was war and no accountability would ever be required nor expected.

Our latest position was now quite close to the Rhine and fortified with many pillboxes (as they were called) spread out over the landscape. For those that don't know what a pillbox was, they are concrete structures set into the ground with slit like openings to observe and through which weapons could be fired without one exposing any of their body. On the negative side these pillboxes could become a death trap if targeted by a tank, bazooka, or a flame thrower. So being assigned two platoons to cover this extended line really made big gaps in our ability to resist what was coming. Our platoons were under the command of a Lt. Michael Buck who was with us (in the general area) and for a while had a jeep to check up on the various positions set up to counter enemy patrols. The jeep would always try to move quickly staying near any houses or trees for best cover. Although Lt. Buck and his aide kept in touch by radio with his superiors several kilometers to the west it was next to impossible to relay any information to us as we were scattered widely. The jeep, when it could circulate without danger, was our only voice contact.

At headquarters the war is played out over maps, large billboards and with pointers focusing on lines that represent military positions. But let me tell you as one who was there that all the talk we got gave little comfort to those of us "boots on the ground" being shot at and watching our own getting killed. War movies never showed the grim reality of what I was exposed to; a small group of inexperienced riflemen being dropped off in a tiny village with not much food, limited ammunition and seemingly being forgotten about. After being dropped off I don't remember anyone saying, Good Luck when they departed. We definitely needed much more than luck as it turned out.

In the early morning hours of January 5, 1945 it seems the Germans were through fooling around with sending small patrols and maybe us too. Someone in our platoon thought they saw flares in the sky early that morning which could have been their signal to move against us. From their direction it started to get real noisy and about to get pretty ugly. Noises we heard were still some distance away but seemed louder over the morning quiet. There was nothing we could compare it to but our guess was their mechanized equipment was being prepared. It was also perhaps a bad omen when the few remaining inhabitants of the village ,bundled up, started running to the nearby woods carrying only the barest essentials. The poor bastards living a simple existence now had this to put up with. The morning was bitterly cold in what turned out to be the worst winter in 25 years.

The jeep was sent out to make the rounds and assess the situation. First on the list was to check out farther towards the river and our guys stationed in those pill boxes. As the jeep approached they were met by our GI's who were now being fired upon and left the pill boxes briefly to talk to us. There message was this place is going to be overrun and we should get the hell out quickly. Several of them were prepared to return to the pill boxes but the jeep driver said maybe that was not a good idea. Further, we could show more resistance from the houses back in the village. Given the shooting close by it didn't take long to change their mind and they started to run towards us. The jeep loaded what it could but those unable to get on managed to get back to our side of the village outskirts. We all sought direction from the CO where to go. The Germans were getting organized now on our side of the Rhine with a large force and would shortly inflict some pain. Given our situation we all had our orders to hold and positioned ourselves as best we could to do what we could.

Before long we could see columns of infantry coming our way in an open field. While at some distance they made little effort to conceal their movements. Many of couldn't help but wonder if we only had some heavy weapons maybe we could have inflicted a little pain on them. Wishful thinking. Behind the infantry and further back their heavy stuff was preparing to move also. They were being kept at the ready and could be moved quickly if the need arose. Even though we were inexperienced in war it became obvious this action was no longer just a patrol; their numbers were much greater. They did not come charging at us shooting ,but rather, they moved methodically in our direction as though no one was in their way. At the same time their greater numbers allowed them to spread out and move widely against our flanks in both directions. Their moves were slow, coordinated and aimed at positioning for advantage. Here, their experience showed, for little shooting started until they were in a position to make it effective. All we could do for the moment was wait.

Being new at this we might have started our shooting much too soon, from too great a distance, perhaps revealing a weakness. Most startling to us was with their superior firepower why no artillery was used prior to the attack startup. They could have really did a number on us and we would have no way to respond anyway! Our thinking was artillery would be an announcement as a prelude to infantry movements so was not done On the other hand, artillery would be more effective against armor which we did not have. From their earlier patrols they probably already assumed all we had was small arms weapons and could only offer little resistance. As we found out later, the noises heard earlier was artillery and other heavy stuff directed closer to the town center a short distance away. The German bridgehead across the Rhine was aimed not only on our village of Gambsheim but on four or five others nearby. Artillery noises we heard most likely were also concentrated on Offendorf about six kilometers away. Our own artillery that might have helped us some was still among the missing.

In the beginning of the ensuing skirmishes some of us could take cover in buildings but in short order that seeming advantage soon evaporated. Buildings were good cover against rifles and machine guns but not their heavy stuff. Lt. Buck, our CO, and the jeep driver would usually always be together so it would be at the lieutenants disposal. As we became under attack it became clear of the importance to protect the jeep as long as possible. When it was not being used Sam found a space between buildings near him. For whatever reason Sam and our CO were some distance away on the other side of town and well out of our sight. Regardless of any ones location throughout the village we were all vulnerable. Sam, the jeep driver, for a while would quickly come by and tell us what was going on and drop off some of the remaining bandoliers of ammo but while doing so started to draw fire. This was the only thing with wheels in our small group so it stood out. The Germans correctly surmised his movements would help the resistance and should be stopped. He was now a choice target and before long his jeep was hit and disabled . Sam and his sidekick got lucky for the moment and were barely able to run for cover inside a house. Because of the way we were scattered around, most of the platoon had no way to know we lost our jeep. After the jeep went down then we really couldn't communicate and find out what our platoon's situation was.

UNDER ATTACK

Being spread out over many yards and in small groups of four to six we could only holler to the others sometimes but that didn't always work. Noises around us did not help. We were isolated and with very much uncertainty. The only thing we knew for sure was we were getting shot at by real experts and little by little moving closer. From our positions originally assigned, a lot of us did not have a clear view towards the open field they approached from. Those that did have a view hollered to us to move closer, find some cover if possible and provide more firepower. Myself and two others went up on the roof of the house we were in to do just that. From here we did get a clear view of their approach and see well into the distance. It seems the roof idea was being done by others several houses away. On the right a small group of soldiers, maybe about six or seven, was seen moving along a fence ahead of the main body. We could see them from the roof but our buddies on the ground could not. There was an old building like a barn they were trying to get to. I don't think they spotted us on the roof. We squeezed off a few quick shots with one going down, another maybe hit and wounded, the others seeking cover. Our guys on the ground couldn't see this group and were wondering what the shooting was about. After a short while they could be seen making their way back to their main group using the little cover available. Getting on the roof proved useful for now but any advantage would be short lived. They would soon figure out where those shots were coming from and make it uncomfortable to stay there. That one small group we were able to see easily but there had to be others around because we could hear sporadic shooting in other parts of the village. It wouldn't be long before they'd return in strength. With just a few houses around good cover was hard to come by. This cover and the roof seemed to work for a while though and slowed them down but the odds were against us for it appeared their numbers were noticeably on the increase. Some of us on the roof worked our way down to the upper floor and moved to a different side of the house. Here we could view a different approach of the open field and back to the tree cover in their direction. It was so hard to know where our guys were and how the enemy was moving. Even though they had to move through an open field with some tree cover the firing at us was enough to disturb reasonable return fire. Their overwhelming numbers allowed them to put up withering fire and allow infantry advancement.

The enemy, as said, had superior firepower and much more of it with tanks soon to follow. This firepower of their infantry contained an extremely rapid fire hand held machine gun (some called it a machine pistol) that became affectionately known as a " burp gun. " The name was derived because when fired sounded like a loud and long belch. Regardless, its sound was terrifying and deadly. Well so much again for our intelligence that forecast we

116

would be only facing patrols. In our area near Gamb-sheim we wondered how come no word of this attack in strength was never passed on to us. In retrospect, however, even if it was it would have made no differ-ence on the outcome. I guess they did the best they could with available troops and spread us way out ac-cordingly and hoped for the best. Like some things in life it would be said that we were in the wrong place at the wrong time. This blitz into our orphan regi-ments overwhelmed our large thinned out sector. As we learned later all three regiments faced the same difficult combat conditions and suffered accordingly. The German assault in strength seemed to be aimed at the sectors covered by our regiments. A write up about my company's platoons facing "Operation Nor-dwind" in particular stated; ....".and so the excruciating conditions were created for the trials of Task Force Linden: overextended, without integral artillery and engineers, regiments displayed under command of other divisions or in special task forc-es, battalions often fractionated from regiments and companies from battalions. And for the first shock, those conditions were compounded by that constant, maddening factor of reshuffling movement. The deck was especially stacked at Gambsheim" **.

** *Excerpts from the 42nd Rainbow Division Newsletter, Reveille, June 2006.*

Later on we did find out American recon patrols had reported boats and other activity in our sector of the Rhine. This meant the Germans moved quite a lot of equipment and men at night and had to cross a river besides. We had no way to know who received such information or what they did with it if anything. Here again we can only think about what might have happened if only we had artillery or even air support. I would think they 'd be vulnerable when crossing a river. But from the hell we were now facing it must fallen on deaf ears and felt of little importance. It didn't take much imagination to realize that infantry at my level was considered of little importance; and maybe not even just another little line on a map. ......" Many veterans of Task Force Linden could testify to the concentrated German firepower at Gambsheim. They underwent their baptism of fire there in hastily formed combat groups that moved against the bridgehead from the south and west . (The thin defensive line of the 232nd in this sector had felt the fury some hours before.)" *

Our CO,(army talk for Commanding Officer) Lt. Buck was in charge of issuing orders when he could. After losing the jeep there was no way to communicate to our various locations. From our positions we were able to slow them down in the beginning for we had some cover where theirs was limited. At

118

this time some of our guys were still using the roof and windows of other houses. Because of this determined resistance we all knew it wouldn't be long before more firepower would be used. Little by little, they moved ahead and we shot when and where we could and by moving around from the few different locations we had. When they got close enough they set up machine guns (which we didn't have) in three locations so matters would only get worse. This was a huge difference so we quickly abandoned the roof but any decent cover choices were rapidly dwindling. Now trying to run to different positions became far more dangerous than before but we continued for a while when we thought it would provide better sighting. It was later we found out those killed were caught in the open or trying to change positions. It's not like we scrambled to other positions on a whim but because the Germans kept moving around causing us to rethink where we were. It didn't occur to us then but this moving around and firing from many different positions slowed them down because our enemy probably thought we had a larger force than we really did. We only moved around a lot to keep from getting hit or to improve our sighting capability. They must have been told what to expect and apparently were being deliberate to see our response. I'm sure what firing we did showed them all we had was small arms and could not cause any great damage. They

119

only held back slightly and cautiously to make this assessment and would make their major push soon.

With their greater numbers their infantry columns could be seen moving widely out and working their way towards and around us. In the early hours when the attacks first started we had only to concentrate in mostly one direction. As time went on and they continued towards and then around us it became real difficult to gain position. Our village and field positions were now being challenged more directly as they moved slowly towards us. It wasn't long after that it was obvious we were now surrounded and as expected both sides were taking casualties, both dead and wounded. We tried to be very careful when shooting not to hit our own guys for they could be anywhere. Words moved along that Lt. Buck took a bullet from a machine gun burst in the leg (some word spread he got hit in both legs) and was down while several others with him were killed outright. We quickly would lose about half our men, killed and wounded, in just the first four hours (not known until after capture). The medic gave him a shot of morphine and dressed his wound with sulfur drugs (standard treatment at that time). I should say here that Medics, men trained to treat wartime trauma in combat, are assigned to infantry and other front line units. Much has been written about their bravery in combat, all of it well deserved.

We already knew from information passed around that we could expect no help requested earlier from the outside and were ,indeed, on our own.. If all these things weren't bad enough think how we felt when tanks appeared from the tree line and were moving our way. Their infantry had bazookas now set up and aimed in our direction. Some of our guys, trying once again, took positions in the upper floors of the houses for a better view but a few rounds of bazookas and 88mm's convinced them otherwise and quickly took care of that. It would fair to say we lost a few more in that exchange. Again daydreaming about what if we had our own heavy stuff could the outcome have been different. We'll never know . Rifles against tanks makes for a very uneven playing field. We were being beat up pretty good. History of the war proved without much question that Germany's 88 mm's, tank mounted, were one of the most feared weapons. Think about this. Germany up to now has been fighting on many fronts for about five years. After all this time they could still produce serious armor to use against us while our own country could provide next to none . However you slice it not a good circumstance and shameful.

Our small and difficult village fighting in our zone (we were to find out later) apparently was also going on in others nearby villages called Sessenheim, Illsburg and Killstett by other elements of our regiment. Our three regiments, the 222nd, 232nd and 242nd were dubbed "Task Force Linden", and yes, were very green and viewed by us as "orphans" because most of us felt abandoned, were left on our own with little firepower, didn't get much direction, support when needed or supplies. Our resistance to their offensive, as screwed up as it was, was given some proper credit in later years and caused their offensive to slow a bit. This was probably a belated military public relations stunt to offset us being used as cannon fodder. The price was high for in January alone the "orphan regiments" suffered 1,483 casualties[*].

Our situation, by now, was to say the least, very bleak. We were now, since the German patrols started, here for over four days, had very little food and down low on ammunition. From what little communication we had, it was presumed we lost over half our men. Trying to communicate with those still alive was difficult because all open areas were now under heavy gunfire. if someone tried to run to another house it would bring an instant burst. One of the worst situations was that our only medic could not know who needed help or get to any wounded. We were in every

---

[*] *Excerpts reprinted by permission of the VFW Magazine, January,1995 & March, 1995.*

sense helpless and, in fact, surrounded. From the German side it might have been somewhat obvious that since our rate of return fire was diminishing could mean that we were running low on ammunition and/or there were less of us still around or able to shoot. Both of these unfortunately were true but it was the ammo problem that was the worst and as learned earlier we would get no help from the outside nor should we expect any. Whether we could have conserved our ammunition or used it differently we would probably never know for sure. Us survivors fought the war as best we could without direction and now had to face the next reality. This is the way things played out for us right or wrong. For my part, I and the few others with me nearby had no more ammunition; a difficult and desperate situation to describe. We did think about others in our platoon, maybe those killed, might still have ammunition but it was difficult to know where they were. Trying to get to that ammunition, if it existed, could also be deadly. The Germans were now close and around us so to try running across an open area to other houses would almost be suicidal. We now had nothing to fight with. Being still cold and hungry and with the enemy closing in our feeling of hopelessness could not get much lower.

The way our platoons were scattered throughout the village of about twelve to fifteen houses and some in nearby wooded areas our Lieutenant did not know our true losses. It was a fair assumption the truth was not good. Our position was now determined to be hopeless and to prevent further bloodshed Lt. Buck arranged for a non-com to go out under a white flag to arrange for our surrender. To show good faith the non-com was accompanied by the medic with a red cross on his arm. There was no doubt we were now completely cut off and surrounded while their numbers and armor around us continued to increase. Our surviving group was told later that Lt. Buck informed Headquarters of our vulnerable position and intent to surrender. History did not reveal how this was received at Headquarters. And since much of the same thing was happening over a large area we wondered what alarm bells were being sounded. Surrendering is a most difficult and scary thing to do for we could never know if they would deal in good faith or just shoot us. When we first arrived in the Strasbourg area we were made aware of and reports circulated that the Germans had earlier killed some American prisoners. This late in the war Germany must have been straining at all levels. With diminishing resources and manpower, taking prisoners might have been frowned upon and would only complicate operations increasing the strain. The reported killing of American prisoners took place in a town called Malmedy ; I never found out where that was but the incident was a historical chapter in this war.

But along with staring down the barrel of the tank's 88mm's, bazookas and looking at several machine guns we didn't have the luxury of many options. It took several trips to coordinate how things would go down but an agreement was made. A squad of Germans returned to face our Lt. Buck and uttered, " Waffen niederlegen! " ; (throw down your arms) and," Hande hoch!" (raise your hands), before being moved to their position. We were also to learn later that Lt. Buck before getting hit had asked for artillery and/or air support but we got neither. Our intelligence, as it turned out, was way off the mark and our platoons had to face the impossible task of holding off at least a battalion size strength of soldiers with tank support and for which we could offer no sustained resistance so our fate was sealed firmly and quickly. It was aggravating to realize that after our training (even though short) how quick our combat role was to end. There was little doubt that the decision by our CO to surrender was not known to those furthest away from our location. This part of the process could prove to be delicate for how could they know? A possible sign to them might be the reduction or outright stopping of the shooting. We hoped the others would surmise something was happening and held our collective breath. If some GI not aware took it on himself to continue shooting could get us all killed.

The process required us to leave our weapons where we were and to move out into the open and away from the houses, hands in the air. Orders were given to move against a row of fences and not move. They quickly moved a machine gun and set it up towards us. All of us thought we would be gunned down then and there. So as not to miss any remaining GI's scattered throughout the village their soldiers moved around under the white flag using the non-com and medic as a shield. If there was any distant holdouts not aware a surrender was being arranged they would have to shoot their own men first. Not too likely. Luckily, the remaining GI's were rounded up, collected and moved to our position along the fence.

After capture we were searched and lined up to start moving us out. There was nothing we could do for our dead but several of us were allowed to help our wounded and others forced to carry dead Germans back with us. Before we left the area our lieutenant asked the German in charge if we could identify our dead. This would require going around placing those "dog tags" mentioned way earlier into their mouths. Permission was granted but had to be done quickly. Our medic was assigned this unpleasant task. With the snow cover and us being tired, cold and hungry made moving their dead difficult. Before long a truck was brought near us to help so we loaded up their dead. Those of our wounded that couldn't walk were allowed to ride along. Up to that time we had no way to know if we caused any real damage to them. I, and I'm sure others, were surprised when being moved back in their direction to see a number of dead ones around the houses and fences with others further back in the clearing. The fallen, ours and theirs, were by now half frozen; not a good sight. We were now seeing there was a toll on both sides; a real grim picture of war for our raw and green eyes. Our wounded along with Lt. Buck before getting on the truck, were taken aside and given some kind of first aid until they could get to better facilities or so we hoped.

They moved us back to a point from their line perhaps a kilometer or so and then stopped. We could see there was some confusion as to who was going to do guard duty and provide escort to our next location. Compounding all this, other prisoners were now being brought in from our other two regiments for they had gone through the same similar and stretched out conditions that we faced. After talking with some of them, their baptism of fire also against really tough odds paralleled our own experience. Further shame on those that brought this on so many of us. From the book "Hold At All Costs", it was reported that almost all of the 42nd divisions POWs till the war ended were captured in their first month of combat.

It took a while but the Germans came to terms with prisoner authority and we were assigned a group that would be our guards at least for the time being. From our location the only way we could be moved was to march on mostly dirt roads. It was still bitterly cold and our boots (called shoe pacs) were developed to combat the cold but were definitely not for walking any distance. These boots were not tightly fitted so any marching at all was sure to cause blistering. We were forced to walk at a fast pace to put some distance between what was our line and theirs. I don't remember how far we went but we soon found ourselves back at the Rhine then loaded into rubber boats and taken across. It was not an easy task but we had to help carry dead Germans, wounded Americans and some heavy equipment into the boats and across the Rhine. Altogether we had to make several trips to move everything. We were being assembled and lined up again to march when once again ugly things happened.

We found ourselves on the receiving end of an American artillery barrage causing everyone to seek cover quickly. This was a surprise for our own (42nd div artillery) was still in transit so this had to be the work of some other nearby division. Wasn't it nice of them to help, well intentioned, but not welcome at this time. It was difficult to find suitable cover being very much in the open, we could not know how the target area was to be swept and was very scary. We didn't dwell on this and dived for cover like everyone else and prayed. It wouldn't matter where you were for if you were close to where the shell landed forget about it. On the receiving end of an artillery barrage, if you are anywhere near the landing area there is no noise until just before impact. There aren't too many ways to describe the chaos of a saturation barrage. This kind of support we could have used a few days or even a few hours ago so it was way too late for us. Our war was now over. Now we had a chance to get killed by our own military and would be written up as just another case of wartime accidents. This description would fit a term that became popular much later and referred to as " friendly fire". That's assuming it would be written at all. There's no doubt many ugly things of the ground war never found it's way into print. I never found out how or when the term " friendly fire" originated but it sounds swell and has a good ring to it.

The barrage caused widespread scattering very quickly so many were out of sight of one another. There were casualties on both sides but we never had a chance to check out those from our side for we had to move out quickly as soon as the barrage stopped. Medical help was brought in for them as soon as it was felt safe to do. Medics usually travel with combat troops. I would think the Germans must have wondered why our commanders allowed artillery to be used targeting areas where prisoners may be present. These thoughts occurred to me so why wouldn't they occur to those requesting artillery fire? Again, was this a lack of communication, nobody cared, or another example of wartime confusion. Remember, Lt. Buck did advise Headquarters of his intention to surrender himself and the surviving GI's. During WWII casualties from accidents and friendly fire were kept quiet for quite a while and most likely even years. By this time, our feet were wet and cold and developing blisters for there was no time to get warm or dry out. When things quieted down we were rounded up and forced to keep moving to put distance between us and the front, wherever that was.

At the end of this day it was now about 48 hours since we had anything to eat, still marching and with no obvious place to settle for the night. I'm not sure how many miles we walked but it was difficult without any food. We were now in a wooded area with no buildings nearby so they confined us in groups and made us sleep outside. Huddling was our only way to keep a little warm. It was apparent to us with this late in the war that their resources were strained at all levels. Their own citizens, understandably, would be given better treatment than us. They got us assembled early in the morning and again we marched for another day with a few rest stops. Most of this day we moved through hilly and heavily wooded areas well known as the "Black Forest", (Schwartzwald) a pretty part of Germany but showing scars of the war. In the early evening we stopped and were herded into an enclosed compound surrounded by wire and guard towers. It didn't take long to see we were being placed in a Russian prisoner camp. At the time it was more important to get out of the weather. The barracks were very much open to the weather but provided some protection, however slight, from the cold..

There were quite a few Russians here and kept separate was a small group of British officers. We were dead tired with sore feet but felt a little relief to get indoors for a change and finally given something to eat. It was here that they handed out a bowl and spoon and told us to keep them. Our meal was a loose cabbage soup and one slice of black bread, not much but was indeed welcome. We didn't know it at the time that this meal was to become essentially our "staple" with a few variations for the duration of our prisoner stay. Word came that we would certainly be moved again very soon after preparations to handle us arrived. Getting to dry off was important and to look over our damaged feet. Everyone had blisters and spent time rubbing their feet to

131

help the circulation badly needed. It was difficult to get our feet to warm up for our housing " accommodations" had little warmth. Keeping warm would turn out to be another of the difficult things during imprisonment.

12

THE AGONY OF PRISONER LIFE

After two nights there we were moved away by marching for a time then for a while in trucks to get us some further distance from their "front". Right after capture we were searched for weapons but our captors let us keep some personal items such as rings, watches, pictures, etc,. We as a group had little money, if any. The trucks kept moving us throughout the day and through several towns where the civilians, many but not all, showed their displeasure towards us. Not unusual given that by now a lot of Germany was in ruins and highly visible. The driver when away from the towns would allow for pit stops. I couldn't be sure how far we traveled but by evening arrived at a camp. Again my memory is hazy but I think this camp was in Baden-Baden.

For a few nights here they put us up in what appeared to be stables with large openings and where there was little protection from the cold. It was still quite cold as we are talking about the German countryside in January of 1945. All this was made worse because when captured we couldn't take along anything extra. There was to be no fire for us and we had to sleep on boards covered with straw. No food was given until the third day. Again, this consisted of a very light soup although this time it was made of rutabaga skins (similar to a turnip) , one slice of black bread and little else. We had surmised, the Germans had developed many varieties of soup for their prisoners from what might normally have been thrown away. So much again for the Geneva Convention! This camp, like the other, had Russian and British prisoners in segregated compounds but for us Americans this was only a temporary stop. The guards let us know we would be moved and fairly soon. During the stay those seriously injured from walking or otherwise sick were moved out presumably for treatment or so we hoped. Complaints to the guards about treatment of our sick was not negotiable. We would not know their fate because we never heard about them one way or another. After four days the guards told us to prepare to move. What a joke, that wouldn't take long because all we had was already on us.

Early one morning we were moved outside and lined into columns of five. Our prisoner group was growing in size many for the same reasons we got captured. It seems, like us, small groups of infantry from our other regiments were also easily overrun by larger forces. We again marched until early afternoon and ended up at a railroad station. After a few hours here a passenger train arrived. The last couple of cars were the famous (or infamous) 40&8's into which we were loaded. These cars bore the marks of war for all showed that at some time they were strafed by our planes. From what we observed when boarding, the cars were not marked so as to alert allied planes that prisoners were on board. Maybe the roof was marked, which we couldn't see, but we didn't think so. With all the bullet holes around us, this again, was not a comforting situation. I often wondered why the Germans would play games with us at stake. On the plus side since we had to be moved, this way would be better than walking. Remember, we were wearing those lousy shoe-pacs and our feet were wet and sore. The largest portion of this train was for civilian or even military transport. From the air there would be no way to distinguish differences so it would be fair game. They packed us in so tight, maybe 50 to 60 in a space designed for 40, so we would mostly stand but take turns squatting. They gave us water in a bucket to drink with another bucket for sanitary use, no heat, and given some packages of cheese and several loaves of black bread to last about three days.

Moving trains in Germany were a tempting target of which we were all aware. Our box cars had small openings (in addition to the bullet holes) through which we could take turns looking out to observe the surroundings even if on a limited basis. When we slowed we knew it was due to passing through a town or even a larger city. The damage from incessant allied bombing was quite evident all around and a testimony to war's ravages. We were again quite lucky to move without getting shot at and arrived at our next stop, Stalag 5A in Ludwigsburg. It was now about January 10th or 11th, 1945. Once again they marched us to the camp some distance from the city, but it appeared to take longer because the guards weren't sure where to go. Any marching at this point was difficult for our bad and wet feet, lack of food and the persistent cold was becoming more difficult to tolerate. A direction was finally determined so off we went and arrived in about one and a half hours. There seemed to be a level of uncertainty where to go until we actually got there.

It was at this camp the Germans separated the officers and non-com's (an army expression to denote non-commissioned officers, mostly those below the rank of 2nd lieutenant) from the enlisted men; a thing the German high command felt appropriate. This, as we found, out was not to be our final destination. This late in the war Germany was mostly on the defensive and the active front was changing rapidly. These events are what caused us to be moved so much. Conditions here were no better than before so we again slept on boards and in pairs to keep a little warm. We were not given a chance or the means to clean ourselves and then it gets worse. The unsanitary conditions, the straw on the boards, and the closeness when sleeping caused our bodies to become infected with lice. With no heat and still quite cold the parasitic lice were also trying to find a warm place from the little body heat we had.

Our food allotment never changed. In the morning we would sometimes get a cup of ersatz (artificial– could have been made from the bark of a tree for all we knew) coffee and a slice of black bread then at night loose cabbage, potato, or rutabaga soup (sometimes with the skins or vegetable itself if we were lucky) and again with the bread. If meat was ever used it made one quick pass through the soup and moved on. Beets were plentiful but saved for a different purpose described later. All of us continued showing signs of weakness and could only think of maintaining our will and develop an attitude to survive. Wherever we stayed the buildings always seemed to be like stables and usually no covers on the openings. No protection from the weather. The terrible conditions of cold, severe frostbite, soup with little solid substance inevitably was taking its toll.

Most of us would suffer from one or more of the following; frostbitten feet, diarrhea, pneumonia, skin ailments and more. As a guess, we would probably be getting less than 130 calories a day.

While here each of us was sent separately to a room where we were interrogated by an English speaking German Officer. Our training drummed into us that in the event of capture we would only be required to give our name, rank and serial number under terms of the Geneva Convention (which, by now, to us was a big joke anyway). All of us thought pressure would be used to reveal more but it didn't happen. We ,least of all, knew very little. They seemed to have knowledge and to know the names and numbers of the Allied armies in their area. While here, the new American prisoners were taken to a room where a member of the International Red Cross (I'm not sure if he was Swiss or French) was presented to this gathering. Postal cards were handed out to be filled in with our home address advising (in French) that I was a prisoner of war. My card was dated January 11 1945 and which I still have to this day. I guess we were now officially a registered Prisoner of War. All of us were now in a fraternity that went by the name," Kriegies" from the German word, " Kriegsgefangener" meaning Prisoner of War.

When the Germans thought we could do some work around the camp they did not hesitate to use us. Some were assigned to keep the latrines (toilets that were no more than a trench in the ground) available for use and to clean them as needed. Others, including myself, were taken to a nearby sugar factory in town that made sugar from sugar beets grown abundantly on surrounding farms. This was not the best place to be for it was quite close to a railroad siding which from its looks had been hit in the past. At this camp we were now some distance from the front and were mostly guarded by soldiers of what was called the "Home Front". These were men judged to be too old for front line service but otherwise providing services to free younger men to carry out the war's deadly combat business.

For us POWs that worked outside the camp we were given an extra bowl of soup as an incentive for others to see. All of us were nonetheless on a truly starvation diet and not in any shape to do meaningful work but occasionally it was tried. I was a prisoner for 113 days and lost about 45 to 50 lbs. which amounted to maybe 30% of my weight. My weight loss was probably about average as we later learned.

After about 9 days here in Stalag VA (5A) Ludwigsburg we were marched back to the railroad yard and once again loaded onto 40&8's box cars. As we loaded we saw this was a fairly long one again with many passenger cars up front with us at the rear. We were jammed with about 50 of us which meant standing for long periods. The guards gave us a bunch of black bread and wedges of cheese (not too generous) and told this had to last for 6 days. We also got two large buckets, one with water and the other for sanitary purposes. We were then locked in.

Some of our travel was done at night wherever possible although much was during the day; always a risky operation. We were very uncomfortable being jammed in and for some reason the train seemed to be jerking constantly. Over the six day trip the train stopped several times due to allied planes in the area as trains always made a tempting target. Occasionally when stopped we were allowed to exit the train to relieve ourselves and empty the honey bucket. As far as we could determine again these trains were not marked to show POWs were on board. We were well aware that this was a long train and our planes would surmise it couldn't be all prisoners. I never found out how the pilots were instructed in cases like this. So not knowing how targets were selected, getting shot at or not became a crap shoot.

Stopping to let us prisoners go into the woods to relieve ourselves seemed to be a chore for the guards so was infrequent at best. The limited food, water, and the cold made for a difficult and stressful journey. Near some city (possibly Frankfort) the train was stopped and the guards took off somewhere not too far away but kept us locked in the boxcars leaving us to wonder what's going on? It wasn't long before we found out. Bombs started to fall not too far away shaking us considerably and then getting hit by some debris. No one in our car got injured and we had no way to know about the others for we lacked communication during the trip. So much for the Geneva Convention again. We were very lucky as it turned out, for we did find out after that this was a major raid on a large and important rail yard.

Some how, after traveling for six days (seemed like 20) and going a distance of only around 300 miles we arrived in what we thought would be our final destination; Stalag III A in Luckenwalde. Moving around to different camps perhaps showed the turmoil within Germany during their final days. Any move no matter how far further strained their available resources. Once again we had to march, hungry and with poor boots, some distance and entered the camp. We were quickly processed and assigned to barracks. Although we spent time in several other camps along the way, here they assigned me a number. I became Prisoner number 200047 and issued a card , which I still have.

141

Our quarters were much of the same with one small difference. In the middle was a small stove and all around were closely fitted bunks. Same as before, the bunks had wooden boards with straw spread around and again with the lice problem. The boards were really hard and since our bodies had little meat left started to cause body sores where contact was made while lying down. After three days, finally something good happened, we and our clothes were de-loused and taken for a shower with lukewarm water, but no soap and no towels. Even so, it felt so good even though we had no change of clothes. This great feeling was a comfort for one or two nights before the lice again made their presence known.

PRISON GUARD TOWER

This was a large camp which held British, Russian, French, Italian, maybe Polish, Serbian, and possibly others all in segregated compounds. Each compound was separated by two strong wire fences topped with barbed wire and with space between. Fences were about 8 or 9 feet high and the space between was for the guards and their dogs to patrol through the many compound areas. Several times a day and at night these spaces were patrolled at fixed intervals. The guards made the rules quite clear; we were not to try getting into other compounds, no communicating across the fences, must be inside our building after dark and no lights to show when the outside camp lights were turned off. When outside though, a lot of communication was attempted across the fences and the guards didn't do much to stop this. At night strong search lights would scan continuously to check for any outside movements. As I recall, the camp was laid out as a large square and at each corner and intervals in between was a watch tower with machine guns.

Our barracks guard, an older man and a member of the home front, became known to us as "Gus" (as I recall). Gus was a fair man who treated us good (he couldn't do anything about the food) and was liked by all around him. Gus tried to give the impression he was stern but it didn't come across that way. His age and the war years showed more as despair since his country was in ruins. He spoke pretty good English and it took a lot of talking and prodding to get him to tell us where he learned his English. Maybe it was a bit of irony but we eventually found out that Gus was himself a prisoner in WWI and sent to a camp in England where he spent about two years. By him being a former prisoner himself may have been a reason why he showed some sympathy towards us at times. Other guards we had to deal with for the most part were fair and used the understanding there would be no problems if nothing serious arose. It got to a point that we could try loose humor with them. Some of us told the guards that they were invited to our barracks to have an evening dinner with us. At the administrative level all were officers and here the interaction was different. They were fair but projected an air of disciplined authority and behaved in keeping with their rank and position. Made clear to us was they must always be regarded and addressed as superior. There was no idle chattering here and complaints of conditions went nowhere. These officers were seen most every night during barracks check.

The city near us, Luckenwalde, had a large railroad yard that became a frequent target. We were forced to join work details and provide labor to repair the bomb damage. In our weakened state it was extremely difficult to move twisted rails and replace them. It took three to four times the number of workers and was slower than normal. . After repairs and getting their yard back in service this place would again soon become a target as before. When it did happen, once again prisoners were sent to repeat the process. I must tell you that even with our camp about a half a mile away, being on the ground nearby during a raid is a very scary and frightening experience. Take it from me, you do not want to be anywhere near the receiving end of an aerial bombardment.

Most of us have seen war movies where the planes would line up and make a perfect bombing run; that was Hollywood's version. Bombs dropped from high altitude do not always hit their intended targets. Measurement of success in a raid would be a matter of conjecture. I'd think if the target was hit 50 % of the time the air force could rejoice. Probably the best way to measure success was if the target could not function for a while. In the real world I was in, on one particular run I'm aware of, none of the railroad yard was hit but an adjacent residential area was really wasted causing great civilian losses, both lives and property. That kind of a bombing run gave us in camp food for thought. The work details got a chance to see this firsthand in town and while doing so felt the extreme resentment from the citizens of the town. The guards had to work at keeping the civilians away. Their feelings did get communicated back to us by the guards and lasted for several weeks. We didn't know it then but this type event needed an expression to denote, "unintended consequences" and became known as "collateral damage"; a euphemistic way of expressing the unintended carnage for dead civilians and destroyed property. What a great way of expressing these losses!! This had happened before and in this war would happen again and again many times as a cost of war perhaps more often than we're led to believe.

Our camp, Stalag IIIA was about 30 miles away from Berlin. From here we could see large groups of American planes heading to Berlin and elsewhere. Air Forces losses were quite large because German defenses would go all out to protect their capital even though by now they should know it was for a lost cause. Anti- aircraft protection around other major manufacturing centers was also extensive. We did witness several planes being shot down some distance away but had difficulty trying to see if any parachutes appeared. We do know from other prisoners that quite a few flight crews did make it to the ground and were rounded up. These air crew prisoners were kept at another location in a camp separated from ground forces for some reason we never understood. The POW camps for members of the air corps was called a , "stalagluft".

I don't know how the airplane operations were planned but the Americans were assigned to the more hazardous daylight bombing and the British to night time. It should be obvious that daytime operation was at a much greater risk than night time resulting in huge American losses. I don't know why the Americans drew this lousy assignment; Washington didn't care about losses, didn't want to offend the Brits, so rotten politics as usual. Even so, the raids continued in strength in huge numbers on Berlin and other important cities. A steady stream of replacements apparently filled the need. The written and photographic history of this war showed the colossal damage to European cities.

After being here for about two weeks we settled into our prison camp life regimen if that's what we could call it. The guards didn't offer any information on us moving again so we assumed this is where we would stay. From experiences so far it didn't matter where we were the food and allotment amount never changed. Our daily food ration would essentially be ;

Morning;----one cup of coffee ERSATZ (artificial) and small piece of bread and sometimes cheese.

Mid-day;-----one ladle of soup (rutabaga, cabbage or carrot) with almost no solid content.

Evening;----Small bowl of loose soup and one loaf of black bread to be divided among seven men.

A method was developed for fairness when cutting the bread. The slicing would be done for seven and all pieces were laid out for viewing. As always, the one assigned to cutting the bread would always get the last piece. This method assured he would be quite careful in slicing evenly.

Some days we were taken out on work details in the city or around the camp. It was still very much winter but work assignments outside the camp, among other things, included moving potatoes, carrots and rutabagas from storage bins onto trucks and then back to camp. These would then be brought to the kitchens where our gourmet soups were prepared. Needless to say every attempt was made to steal and hide some but most times were caught without punishment. There were times the guards would be sympathetic and allowed us to get away with it. Other days we would hang out indoors to keep warm, talk about food (always a favorite) and try to guess when we might see the wars ending and to think about being liberated. Although we were kept segregated in compounds by nationality some of the work details allowed us to get close to the others where information could be exchanged. Mind you, this would have to be done very carefully, but was done nonetheless.

For a period of time some from our barracks would get detail assignments near the British compound where information was gleaned and passed on to us. Scuttlebutt (military jargon for rumors) had it that the British had access to a radio that was obviously kept well hidden and quiet. That news pumped us up a bit for all other news got to us haphazardly, didn't know if we could believe it and usually most news was depressing anyway. With this radio they were able to listen to allied broadcasts and get updates on the war's progress (at least from the Allied perspective). There was no reason to believe those broadcasts were not truthful and buoyed us emotionally. Having a radio in a POW camp sounded like a Hollywood war movie. We, of course, were skeptical, didn't believe it, and thought the radio story was a bit far fetched. But rumors persisted and information was smuggled to us as discreetly as possible. This thing about the radio was not exactly a daily conversation topic but would from time to time be heard passing around. Everyone had to make sure the Germans didn't hear anything on this, if they did the consequences would be severe.

Britain was in the war since around 1939 and fought many campaigns against the Germans. Large scale operations took place in North Africa where many prisoners were taken by both sides. This resulted in the Brits becoming long term prisoners and in the process learning better survival skills. As time passed the radio story developed something like this. It seems when an allied bomber was shot down (there were many) it was the British that were called upon to go to the crash site to remove any dead or wounded airmen. While there, a radio savvy prisoner would scrounge for radio parts while his other comrades would cause a commotion about something to distract the guards. Over time enough parts were taken and eventually fashioned into a working radio that could only be run on battery; also gleaned from the crash site. This scenario seemed quite reasonable and slowly started to sink in to us so we became believers and put some faith into the feedback. Because we didn't have too many good things to talk about the radio scuttlebutt buoyed us and gave us some hope. Hope was generally in short supply.

As the days and weeks went on with our meager daily food ration we got thinner and weaker. By now I think we were approaching a point where our weight would taper off and stabilize. During basic training all of the recruits were taught that in the event of being captured we would be treated in accordance with the Geneva Convention. As such, we would receive one Red Cross package per man per week. The difference of what we were supposed to get versus what we got was laughable to the extreme that we could easily die as a prisoner. Many of us did. For basic survival we had to take chances whenever an opportunity presented itself even with serious risk involved. We started to do things going against everything the guards told us not to do, it's called desperation.

The British and French prisoners in our camp were long term in capture because they were at war with the Germans long before the USA got involved. Their long time captivity, it seemed, allowed them privileges not available to other nationalities. However they did it, they all physically looked way better than us. The Brits were given the task of establishing a protocol for prisoner handling, to generate rules and to teach some basic discipline throughout the camp. This probably from their heyday of empire building and territorial conquests. The French because of their reputation served in the kitchen where the terrible soups and black bread was prepared. I wouldn't think the French would want to boast about this food but I guess they were only working with what was given to them. These privileges must have paid off for these two groups looked far healthier than the rest. Even the long time Russians looked better than us. This let many in our compound to suspect these others had more and better food than us but we couldn't figure why. It was not easy to get answers on any food related issues so it was dropped and forgotten.

Most of the Russians were also long time prisoners. The bad blood between the Germans and Russians is well known, goes way back in time and carried over to this war. I am no historian but the terrible fighting in Russia was almost always to the death and few prisoners were presumed to be taken. From our experience being in other camps there were quite a few prisoners we observed. Without knowing exactly, this number had to be in the thousands. With this background they were given many dirty job details but apparently managed to get adequate food for their effort because they looked better than us. Many of us surmised that the longer you were a prisoner the better you could learn the skills of survival. Another factor we felt late in the war was perhaps they kept the Russians somewhat fit in case the Russian Army were first to liberate. In that event, if the prisoners looked emaciated the guards would probably be dealt with harshly. This kind of thinking, however, didn't explain why us Americans were allowed the barest of food provisions and all of us showed it. If there was any logic to the Germans plan to keep us emaciated it surely escaped us. This was a favorite topic and discussed often. A leading consensus developed about this and centered on the fact that the United States had no business fighting against Germany. The reason being Germany's politics on territory should have only resulted in European concerns.

Our compound had the French on one side and the Russians on the other. As mentioned earlier when first captured, we were allowed to keep (or hide as best we could) personal items such as rings, watches, cigarettes, neck chains and things like this. With us as new prisoners, we were expected to have some personal items. So the French and Russians made it clear to us during our walks near the fences, that they were in a position to barter bread and other foods in exchange for our personal items. Bartering has been done in this camp for a long time as we learned from the Brits. That was as long as one had something to barter. When all personal items were gone then there was nothing to offer. Language difference was a little problem but each side made their intentions known with hand gestures. Among us Americans there was usually some that spoke reasonable French, but rare to speak Russian. All we could hope that any agreement undertaken would be honored for there was no way to complain or for recourse. Even worse, we were now actually getting involved doing things strongly advised against. Desperation overcame one of our GI's to the point that he actually tried to cross the barbed wire area and was shot and lasted only about two hours. It seems from conversation he was bartering with the French for bread. Tragic, so close to the war's end but unknown to us then!!!

The bartering system(for lack of a better term) would work something like this. While outside walking around our compound and near the fences the nearby French or Russian prisoners who had anything to sell would try to make eye contact. By using hand signals and fingers we would get the message that something like a wrist bracelet or neck chain could bring in 4 or 5 potatoes or a head of cabbage. We preferred bread but this would require giving up rings, watches and even cigarettes. Cigarettes were always in short supply but those that did have them were careful to keep it quiet. The only other source of cigarettes was in the Red Cross packages we were supposed to get. In my 113 days as a POW I received only three or four boxes and each one had to be shared four ways. It was at this time the first of our Red Cross packages were distributed to us but had to be shared as above mentioned. The bartering thinking was set aside for a while but would be restarted when needed.

The idea of trading personal goods was made not without some conscious thought. It didn't take long to figure the jewelry was of little value if we died here. The biggest weight loss occurred in about the first five to seven weeks, after that it slowed down for our bodies had less and less by then to give up. So to make a deal we thought about it for a while then agonized a little bit but not for long. If we went ahead and bartered and gave up our jewelry we could not know if they (the foreign POWs) would hold up their end of the "arrangement". We could not be sure about an "honor" system. But survival is a really strong emotion and ultimately overshadowed all other considerations. A ring could usually be traded for three, maybe four, loaves of bread while a watch might bring six or seven. Being the newer prisoners there we could not know if that would be a fair exchange or should we ask for more. Feedback from others indicated the amount could go up or down a little but the deal was close to the going rate. Each individual had to decide if the amount was worth it. Once an arrangement was made the actual exchange might be considered a work of skill but with potentially severe consequences.

Since it was the other foreign prisoners who had something we wanted we had to make the first move. Our item to be exchanged had to be wrapped in paper or cloth or whatever we could get our hands on. It was also advisable to get some small rocks to add a little weight. The exchange would be made when the night sky was close to darkness in hopes we would not be seen by the guards. Those of us involved would get near the fence and after making the usual hand motions to verify amounts would toss the item over the two separated fences and hoped it would land correctly. The prisoner in the adjacent compound would check to see if he had the right item and if all appeared well the bread would similarly be tossed into our compound one loaf at a time. As you can imagine we had to be quiet doing this so as not to attract attention. This bread made life a little better for a while but even with some self rationing it would be gone and we pondered what the next move might be. The conditions of our existence day to day never changed, were severe and with little hope for improvement. . We were not much more than skin and bones without adequate food and poor clothing and being in the middle of a difficult German winter slowly continued to take it's toll.

Late afternoons before darkness all of us had to assemble outside and a head count was made. While here, our barracks was inspected to see if any monkey business was going on that they should know about. Items we collected from bartering had to be well hidden. This was definitely not allowed as we were told early on. But many of us did wonder if the guards knew this activity was being done and chose not to fuss about it. In any case, tips on hiding from the Brits came in handy as they had learned from experience. The head count and inspection was a daily event. It was at this time if things checked out to the guard's satisfaction we would get our meager evening soup and bread allowance. During our inspection I kept thinking about the Brits with their radio and how it was concealed. I guess they had plenty of time to figure a workable solution.

Stories of escaping from a POW camp are available and supposed to be based on factual information. I'm sure some actually happened. The notion of escaping from a POW camp is best handled by some movie maker who doesn't have a clue as to the reality of what it was like. In our case each of the compounds were double fenced, were patrolled by guards with dogs and had guard towers with machine guns to cover a wide view. We did not have access to tools and the barracks, as mentioned, were inspected daily. Beyond that, the even bigger drawbacks were the cold conditions, language, frozen ground, no food to carry and worst of all our weakened and emaciated state. Keeping us in this condition might have been a German military strategy but somehow didn't jibe with our observations of the other prisoners.

My memory of some war movies and later TV programs about American POW's in Europe was that they were a happy lot well fed and had fun trying to outsmart their captors. One big happy family but laughable by what we were experienced. Escaping prisoners in movies I have seen appear to have not missed a square meal. By estimates in a VFW magazine, September 2005, the survival rate was 25 to 1. From the same source there were 93,941 American POWs (Europe) and 1,812 successful escapes; less than 2.0%. Using these same numbers means about 3,760 POWs died while in captivity.

This late in the war the Germans must have known or certainly suspected they were fighting a lost cause. It also must have been made known to them American POWs might possibly become bargaining chips useful during surrender negotiations. This wouldn't work as we knew later because the Allied Command would accept nothing less than unconditional surrender. None of these presumed strategies did anything to improve our existence so the soup and bread continued. We knew the civilians were living on less and less and were pretty war weary. During some of our out of camp work details you could see the despair in their eyes and could tell they were preparing for the inevitable and maybe hoping it would be soon. Near the war's end, there was no let up from the air nor the constant assaults of the ground war.

War news continued to be circulated by the British but, as said, always carefully. It was now into Early March and we could only hang on as best we could but for how long was always a question. By now I must have lost about 50 lbs., which we would find out later, was sort of an average for our group and represented 30% of my body weight. While spending time in the barracks we often wondered after liberation how could the German Authority ever reasonably explain our poor condition. When the time came, it would be beyond any reason how they could possibly explain a believable response.

Our camp was close enough to Berlin so we could see and often hear the constant air raids trying to break the will of their people and the back of their industry. Neither did we have to be reminded of our proximity to the Luckenwalde railroad center where we often worked and could get wiped out and who would know. Remember earlier, not all bombs or even artillery hit their intended targets. Air raid frequency seemed to increase and continued in quantity and, as usual, prisoners were sent as work details to repair damage. In our weakened state it would take at least four times the manpower usually required. In our own way we had little desire to get their railroad up and running. This , I'm sure, they already knew. Results from us prisoners was not good enough, took too much time, so local civilians were brought in to assist and quicken the pace. Keeping the railroads running was naturally a high priority. In our prison camp world the best we could do was to monitor all events and keep our hopes up that soon this would end and we would be back in friendly hands. Living conditions and work assignments for the next four weeks continued without much change, just more of the same. What did change was we could only do less and less. It was a real challenge to get the energy to do anything but we had to try. Understandably, this was always with us.

13

THE JOY OF LIBERATION

It is now into mid- April and rumors are becoming more frequent throughout the camp. There is great concern as to who will actually show up at our camp first. The Allies are closing in mostly from the South and West. The Russians are rumored to be moving in quickly from the North and East. There is a lot of confusion among our guards for, unless they are in complete denial, they must know their cause is finished and the end is quickly approaching. I am also quite sure that all the guards had no desire to get killed now for that would change nothing, certainly not the war's outcome.

The strong drives by the Allies and the Russians are now creating new problems. As they advance, the POW population from other camps are being moved around and into our camp causing overcrowding far beyond our already bad situation. We were already on starvation rations and concerned about how they could possibly reduce it.. Noticeable was the number of guards at our camp seemed to vary day to day but we didn't know if that had meaning. We guessed it might be another indication of confusion, their desperation, or more importantly, whose side they would rather be captured by. It seemed to be very clear the last thing the guards wanted was to be taken by the Russians where old scores could be settled and for which they would like to avoid . Our guards would not wish to show these types of weaknesses but it came through to those that knew them best; the long time prisoners.

As strange as it may seem the large Russian POW group in our camp was showing both joy and concern. It was widely believed when Germany invaded Russia that Russia's soldiers would never surrender and would rather die than become a German prisoner. Nevertheless, for whatever wartime circumstances took place, Germany had taken many thousands of Russian prisoners. A popular notion within the camp circulated among us was that the Russians now doing the fighting might look upon the Russian POW's held by the Germans as possible deserters and could be put through a difficult and unpleasant interrogation.

The amount of guards present continued to change almost daily and apparently had something to do with moving POWs from eastern stalags. As expected, another groundswell of confusion showed up again. It was at this time we started to get a few more Red Cross packages than we saw for the last two months. Perhaps an indication the end was getting nearer. With us starving and with some local warehouses with plenty of these packages available would present the German authorities with a difficult explanation. To offset a potential embarrassment we heard many of these packages were circulated among the civilians thereby giving the appearance of limited supplies. I didn't understand the German's position on this for certainly the prisoners would give their story when it was their time. Please remember these packages were supposed to be for us prisoners under the terms of the Geneva Convention. When this silly Convention was written, how and by whom did they really expect the terms and conditions to be enforced? Our captors? Did these writers really expect that in an all out and prolonged war honor would be observed anywhere? That ridiculous piece of paper was as worthless then as the United Nations is today. Seems hollow and very naive diplomacy was still alive and well. Whatever was in the language didn't matter for it certainly was not working for us so who do you complain to? Rumors once again moved around the camp and persisted that we could be moved again.

Around April 13 reports started to circulate that President Roosevelt had died. We didn't believe it at first but there was no real reason for them to lie so after a while we accepted it as fact. It turned out certainly to be true. When these Red Cross packages were being distributed we were constantly being warned not to trade with other compounds. While passing these out the guards would punch holes in the cans and sometimes opened other sealed items. This was their way of keeping us from possibly storing them for an escape or to be used in bartering. Rumors continued that we would be moved soon as the Russians were about 20 kilometers away and moving quickly. Another thing that didn't stop was the distant and steady air raids and the sound of artillery getting closer. Activity of some sort was on the rise reflected by the continuing commotion around us. Compounds of other foreign prisoners were emptied and marched off in some cases in the direction of the approaching Russians. Feedback although limited indicated Serbs, Polish and maybe Russians were involved. Our camp was receiving Americans, Brits and French from far away camps. What meager resources the camp had for us was now being strained even further .

On or about April 16th a large contingent of us was told to quickly get ready to make a move. As before, just about everything we owned was already on us so there was nothing to delay us. I think most of us were Americans but as the group developed words spread that many to be added were perhaps Brits and some French. It was difficult to get a straight story. Worst of all, again, there was no transportation so we had to walk. If the Germans had any trucks to spare it was not for us but I guess they had their own problems getting more noticeable by the day. We were so run down it occurred to us we could now die and be left along the roadside. It would appear we were going West to avoid the Russians advancing from the East. We couldn't go very far without resting which was allowed but only in short stretches. Along the way we didn't get much cover as planning was non existent and we often slept outside and in the rain. Care for our well being was just not a consideration. I was not sure how much distance we covered in a day, we knew it wasn't much, nor did it matter for we really didn't know what the plan was, if any. Knowing the war may be over soon gave us the strength to keep moving. This marching went on for about 6 days (I guess, as keeping track of time got to be difficult) as we went through towns with names like; Seyda, Jessen, and Annsburg. For some days we traveled maybe no more than three to four miles just due to the logistics of control over long stretched out columns of us half-humans. Our guards for the most part were members of the "old guard" which meant they were up in age. On this march they had to walk along side us and many showed weariness even though they were better fed. Their energy level, morale and attitude seemed to diminish by the day. On these marches food was brought out by truck so it naturally cooled and was served that way. It was as expected.

The guards changing behavior and frequent huddling did give us the impression that strange things were still taking place and confusion was ever present. When they huddled they surely were talking about what options they had. From the look on their faces we questioned if even they new exactly where we were headed. For the last four or five days many of us got the impression that the guards were simply going through the motions of their job and not watching us too carefully. This late in the war the guards were now, most likely. concerned for their own fate and who could blame them. The number of guards again varied almost unnoticeably from day to day so it was difficult to assess the purpose of what was really going on. When alone many of us discussed escaping but we were very weak, mentally drained and could not summon much strength. Down deep we knew we could not get very far. Furthermore, even with all the daily confusion, our movements seemed to be for the right reasons. Our direction was always towards the Allies and at least we were still getting our lousy soup and bread. All of us were very lean and our stomachs so shrunken that it didn't take much to fill it. If they thinned out the soup even more we would never know it.

Trying to make an escape now didn't make much sense so the consensus of our immediate group was to stay the course so we did. After leaving Annsburg our march continued for a couple more days passing through; Prettin and Dommitszch heading towards the Elbe River and in the general direction of the Americans. Some nights we got under a little cover but that was a luxury so most of the nights we again had to sleep outside. Fortunately, it was now April so the weather warmed up slightly making it a little more bearable. As we got closer to the Elbe River near Leipzig the strange feeling sensed a few days ago got stranger. We continued to go west for another day or so. Now near the end of this trip we were outside and near a town called Krina then led to several large barns, ours for the night and where we slept. Most barns like this had many large openings but offered some protection and better than none at all. After the walking we did, sleeping even with our body lice was not a problem. I wondered if our lice knew they were going on a trip? By now, after being on the road for about a week even our body lice were complaining of hardships. All of us had this problem so we talked of this sick humor as better than no humor at all.

Scuttlebutt circulated that we were now quite close to the Americans. After a day here our guards led us through this town called Krina in the direction of the American lines or so we thought although we could not know this for sure. All of these happenings were vague at best. Part of the way through this town and much of the immediate visible surrounding area were many white flags . In addition were many German soldiers in uniform and even civilians standing around. This was an unusual sight to say the least but most welcome. All around us were our guards that traveled with us but the sounds of war heard just two days ago could not be heard; it was eerily quiet. It appeared that some sort of cease fire might have been arranged, even if temporary, to make a prisoner exchange. This turned out to be an exchange alright but not in the usual sense. As it turned out it seems we were being liberated by a section of the 104th Division that appears to have been waiting for us at the bank of the Mulde River. The whole process was a little weird for it was not what most people would visualize as a "liberation". There was no high ranking German officer with us so an American officer met with a senior guard to negotiate the exchange requirements.

As we crossed the river we were walking into freedom but our German guards, after putting down their weapons, were going with us themselves becoming American prisoners of war. Us half-humans were so overwhelmed with emotion we wanted to cry. The war was not officially over so we wondered why they were giving themselves up, seemingly, voluntarily. Remembering that most guards we knew were of the "old guard" and were fairly sure they had no or little fight left. Many of us thought the faces expressed by the guards were one of relief and glad to put the war behind them. Almost six years of war would wear most people down. At the time it seemed so strange for the actual end of hostilities happened around May 5th or 6th ,1945. I don't think I ever did get an answer to that situation for we were now back with our own so that satisfied us. It was now April 23rd or 24th , 1945.

After the exchange we quickly went through a processing to establish our Army identities, then trucked to a sort of recuperation center where we were given hot rations that we didn't have to share. Our stomachs were so pitifully screwed up it took me close to three days just to start eating again, but gradually. Adjusting to this reality will take a while. Besides our poor physical condition the psychological aspects was more difficult to deal with. While here we got deloused had a shower and even a change of clothes, a most pleasant experience. The long term effects of exposure to lice left all of us with scabies like sores over quite a bit of our bodies. Our Government should have then taken pictures while naked to show the world how we looked. And without question, from our ordeal, just about everyone was also having foot problems now. How all of this would affect us later in life was something we just didn't think about at this time. Our main thought was, hopefully, this would be the beginning of the healing process. The joy going through my mind allowed few other thoughts to exist.

After several days here we traveled by truck to a former Luftwaffe airfield in Halle where again we stayed for around a week while plans were made for our next move. A good size field hospital was set up here with a mess hall to boot. Seems strange, but not really, from force of habit we would grab food and try to hide it. Getting back to normal will take a while. We were all given physical exams and a good amount of time was spent on psychological and military intelligence debriefing. There did seem to be a high level of interest in our stories so we gave lengthy discussions on our prisoner experiences to the interrogating officers. I know I gave them a strong message on, what happened to the Geneva Convention that was supposed to govern our treatment? These officers couldn't or wouldn't offer answers. I'm sure from talking with other POWs they were prepared to do the same. We would never get to know what, if anything, was done with our statements. As we watched for the next few days this hospital had a steady stream of returning prisoners and wounded GI's. to handle. Given its location, this would become a very busy place with each day showing more and more soldiers arriving to process. As mentioned, One thing that should have been done but was not was to photograph us with no clothes. Pictures like that would have made a profound statement for the archives but for some reason was covered up. Like it or not our Government did things that certainly gave the appearance of " selective censoring".

Many of the camps set up in France to process the GI's were named after cigarettes (smoking was very popular in the 1940s). When it was our time to move we were flown on paratrooper transports from Halle, Germany to Rheims, France and then trucked to a camp called; Lucky Strike. These old airplanes with seats stretched along each side were uncomfortable for our skinny asses and were really noisy. For those paratrooper guys comfort was not even a remote consideration. It was a relief when the plane landed and the trip ended. The camp was set up to handle many GI's, was quite large and also had a field hospital and an extended mess hall. Here we were given another physical exam, inoculations to treat our symptoms, got better fed and generally relaxed while plans to move us were taking place.

Not sure of the dates but it seems that us ex-POWs and those wounded slightly were loaded onto trucks and moved to Le Havre, France, a major port, and put on a freighter or transport of some type. Filling up the ship took about three or four days then we left for the good old USA on or about May 1,1945. Again our ship became part of a convoy and had destroyers as escorts. For all of us the trip back might have problems we would rather not think about for the war was still on. All of the wartime shipboard restrictions going over were still in effect. Early in the war, remember, Germany and Japan formed an alliance to fight the western powers. When Germany surrendered unconditionally May 8,1945 we were at sea and the Allies could never be sure if their navy received proper notification or rogue elements would continue to fight on wherever they could. There was no way to tell if the Atlantic was safe for our crossing and our demeanor showed much anxiety and deep concern. Anytime to get killed is bad enough but to face that now after our frightful experience would be unthinkable.

News of the war's end and signing of the Armistice spread very quickly. Allied forces now had the task of winding down and to provide soldiers for the occupation. One of the huge jobs to be done was rounding up and handling German soldiers expected to give up their arms and surrender. Not many people can grasp the enormity of what had to be done. Thousands of American prisoners were being moved to recuperation centers and now thousands of Germans as prisoners also would need processing and care. Winding down a huge war creates mind-boggling logistics. In many areas diehards still offered resistance and might possibly fight to the end. Because of this American soldiers had to be vigilant and operate as though the war never ended. History of the end of WWII recounts how high ranking German Officers including some family members committed suicide. This happened in Berlin, including Hitler himself (with wife/girlfriend) and was perhaps their final act of allegiance.

There were limited medical facilities on board but was adequate to handle the number of cases requiring help. The ship's cargo, us, this time was fragile so we would not have to do much of anything but relax. The trip was laid back with most talk centering on what to do for the future. We encountered bad weather after three days that lasted for another three. After about fourteen days of a fairly routine trip we landed, once again, back in Camp Kilmer, New Jersey on May 15,1945 this time with little regard for secrecy. Entering the harbor all of us were allowed to spend as much time on deck as we cared to.

14

REST AND REHABILITATION (called "R&R")

After arriving at Camp Kilmer mid May of 1945 we
again went through easy daily routines while waiting to find out what the military had in store. About
two weeks went by when orders came to pack our
few belongings and sent us to a beautiful and famous resort in upstate New York called Lake Placid. I considered myself quite lucky for we found out
later other POWs were sent to less desirable locations. What a far cry from the camps used for our
training. It seems the Government took over places
like this one to use for rehabilitation and to prepare
us once again for civilian life or at least that was
our thought. Most of us here were POWs but mixed
in were some soldiers with less severe war wounds.
Maybe it was also viewed as a good will gesture for
what we experienced. Life was really good here, the
scenery was fabulous, we were at several thousand
feet altitude and even without the winter snow the
beauty was all around us. Our messed up mindset
didn't allow us to really appreciate where we were.

Time to make adjustments to reality was still an unknown and would find it's own way.

Spread all over the area were houses mostly like "A" frames built into the hillsides that could be called chalets or perhaps villas where we were billeted about 8 to 10 GIs each. Each of us had our own bunk two in a room which provided good space. As this was an upscale winter resort each chalet had a huge and beautiful fireplace. It was easy to visualize the splendor this place offered in peacetime. Food we would get not far away in a common area mess hall and to us former POWs anything tasted good. It was required to attend several classes a day (a sort of psychological debriefing) but we also had plenty of free time to socialize within the camp and then in the local village although limited. The subject came up and many of us talked about why we were not allowed to visit home before this.

But the truth was we were still openly fragile, in fact and in appearance, and the Government might have been leery of wanting us to be seen in public like that. How long it would to take for our bodies to heal was anyone's guess. Like most returnees we were young and expected to heal quickly. At this point in my life and with what I experienced I was still only three months over my nineteenth birthday!!!!! The cadre here seemed to make veiled suggestions that talking about our experiences before further debriefing was something the military would rather we not do until given a clearance. I can not remember if we were specifically asked not to discuss POW life in public but the camp chatter seemed to suggest it. Still, these thoughts were our take on possible reasons why Uncle Sam was not ready to turn us loose. Here in Lake Placid we did, as mentioned, enter the village and walk among civilians where the local population was not very large in the summer and must have suited the military's purpose.

When the subject of civilian life came up the cadre made it clear that we should not lose sight of and were reminded that a war was still going on in the Pacific. For me, I could not forget that, as I had a brother over there that I assumed was still alive. My other brother in the navy, the oldest one, was still (to the best of my knowledge) in the European Theater for we had long since lost contact with each other. One of my brothers was already in the Pacific so it started to concern me that the navy would shift the other one to that war site. In war anything can happen and they were still at the mercy of the military planners. As I learned very quickly in the past year manpower can be moved anywhere to satisfy a need.

Good things finally happened and for the first time in many moons we could keep company with the village females which we had not had any contact with for so long. Sex was not high on the list, far from it, for most of us were not ready yet, both physically and emotionally. Many of us wondered if the ladies were being friendly because of what we had been through. In this small community with little population the girls were outnumbered heavily by us GI's. Besides, our time here would not be for very long. Activities like bowling, skating, swimming and ping pong we were not up to yet so we just hung out, talked a lot, took in movies and just enjoyed our beautiful surroundings. There was one young lady named Virginia (nickname Ginny) that I was drawn to. One of those things where you just, hit it off, as the saying goes. We seemed to enjoy each others company, had similar interests, and spent time together as well as socializing with her friends. While it was great we both realized that I would soon have to part and go where ordered. We were both very young and much to soon to commit so we parted as friends. For a while we kept in touch but as time passed we drifted away.

Even though some good was happening a lot of my time was spent reflecting on where we had been, what we had been through and to savor what we had now. Still it was really a pleasure being in the company of the opposite sex. Being with the ladies gave us some encouragement that maybe someday normalcy would return to our lives. The POW trauma was constantly in our mind and would not go away easily. We agonized over how our health would be affected in the future. Each of us had to deal with the potential long term effects in our own way. It was viewed then that we would have to depend on Veterans Administrations Hospitals not held in high esteem then. Hope was placed on the old saying that," time heals all wounds".

For quite a while now, we did not receive any pay (for obvious reasons) so it was here we finally got some three months back pay,,,,,,,,,,, whoopee! This was not a lot of money because army pay back then was about $21.00/month and out of that they deducted some for our service insurance and the laundry. At the time I don't know if I checked to see if the Army deducted laundry money. If they did, It would have been wrong (again, for obvious reasons). But so long ago, not much I can do about it. From whatever money received I had to keep some for myself but for the rest of my money I had made arrangements to send it to my family when I found out I was headed overseas. Those were tough years at home and I knew they could use every bit of it. Time passed very nicely here with very little to do except for the socializing which did help in the healing process. Our time here was about two months going through June and July and into early August when I received orders to report to Fort Devens in Massachusetts, my original starting place. I must tell you by now each of us had no desire to leave for we succumbed to this beautiful place, the living style it offered and wished it could be longer. Being here as guests of the U.S. Government placed us into sort of a dream world none of us could ever get on our own. Places like this are the subject of books and writers and afforded only by those of means. This place was set up to process returning soldiers with R&R so we knew we would have to leave to make room for others, albeit reluctantly. It was unfortunate and unwelcome but all good things must come to an end.

I reported to Fort Devens, checked in and assigned to a small barracks. Myself, a few POWs and the slightly wounded were kept here away from the general population. Our group required continuing medical attention and positioned for such. This was still a processing camp for new draftees, like I was, being brought into the Army. Remember, we were told of the war still on in the Pacific so military drafting was ongoing. I was allowed to go home on furlough for three weeks then told to report to Camp Edwards on Cape Cod all very near my home. My time at home couldn't have been better. But while here it was sad to find out the status of who was still in service and those that died serving. At the end of European hostilities about 174,000 serving were killed in action in Europe alone. Like a lot of city neighborhoods just about every young person was in uniform. Still it was great to be home even though I had two older brothers out there serving somewhere. Time passed very quickly while I was home then I was off to Camp Edwards were my next assignment was a bit ironic and beyond belief. What really happened was actually beyond what some movie maker might come up with as a story line.

Camp Edwards was actually a pretty large base for army personnel, as well as, it had an airfield and facilities for the Air Corps (as it was called then). When I arrived I was assigned duties to oversee camp services and in an extreme bit of irony who do you think was doing the work; German and Italian prisoners of war that had been transported all the way to the states. Camp services would consist of just about everything to keep things moving. Supplies for the barracks, toilets, showers, etc., were loaded from warehouses to the trucks and distributed throughout the camp. Also included would be foods and medicines delivered wherever needed. Prisoners did the work supervised by myself and other former POW's. I had difficulty with their good standard of living and carried resent-ment for a long time. Later I learned some prisoners were sent as far west as Utah. It was unbelievable to me and I wondered how many Americans knew that the enemy was in their own back yard. This policy for enemy POWs was not exactly front page news. I can assure you that from my observations the prisoners here were treated far better than what we received in Germany. Myself and other former POWs felt a lot of pain to see how our Government handled this. From my sorry perspective, The Germans and Italians were staying at The Camp Edwards Hilton.

After our liberation and subsequent debriefing we had told the Army how badly we were treated. I know I went into great detail so I assume other POWs did the same. The interrogators showed no emotion and none of what we said seemed to matter to anyone listening. Were talking about thousands of former POW's. For this and other reasons I had a lot of bitterness for many years that kept me from joining divisional reunions and military organizations. I felt a need to separate myself from anything military. These feelings will never leave me. Even though I relented in later years I can never resolve my feelings of how we were thrown out as cannon fodder to the enemy nor our Govern-ments nonchalance to our shoddy treatment.

Much was made of the German high command when put on trial and were to be judged on crimes against humanity. I always wondered if we former prisoners were considered part of this humanity. After quite lengthy trials, well documented, some at high levels, were convicted and executed. Others were imprisoned for life. My feelings were not swayed in the least. It was understood for many years that prisoners of war were to be treated by the covenants of "The Geneva Convention" and monitored by the International Red Cross. None of which happened as seen by my eyes and those of other former POWs. The first sight of returning American prisoners should have raised a huge flag and commotion for the world to see. I don't know if the International Red Cross was ever brought to task. Now that all this was behind me I wonder if this group really existed at all? Back in the story I mentioned that we filled out cards to be sent to our families. This was a notice we were POWs , and although not said, was to be our only communication. Present when this was done was a representative of this International Red Cross, at least that was our understanding. Beyond that, during my confinement I experienced no other contact with that group.

It was now towards the end of August and having been back in the states for about three months many of us wondered why the Army didn't start to discharge us. The answer lied in the fact that the war in Europe was over but in the Pacific things were very much ongoing and from what we were privy to the US was making plans to actually invade Japan. It was not beyond thinking of our Government that even though we had suffered as POWs that we could be used again in combat. If Japan had to be invaded as planned it had been estimated that 250,000 Americans could have been lost. The invasion plan with estimated casualties appeared in the September, 1995 issue of the VFW magazine.

Sometime during the war the United States developed a new super weapon under the most secretive of conditions. It was to be awesome in its destructive capability and something the world had never seen. Fortunately, President Truman had the guts and vision to use this new weapon on August 6th and Aug 9th . which quickly caught their attention. This new weapon an atomic bomb ended the war in Japan saving huge amounts of American lives. Many years after the war there were some Americans (?) who stated we were cruel to use that bomb. For some reason, there were some that worried that civilians , women and children, would be killed. They apparently didn't care how many Americans might die. Stupid people that were obviously never shot at. If I were in charge at that time I would have dropped a few more! I would suggest that these same people consider what might have happened if the Japanese had such a bomb when they bombed Pearl Harbor. No living soul, especially someone that calls themselves an American, should ever second guess that important decision.

15

DISCHARGE AND RETURN TO CIVILIAN LIFE

Because of President Truman's heroic decision the unconditional armistice with Japan was signed on Sept 02,1945 on the deck of the battleship Missouri in Tokyo Bay. Shortly thereafter, around the end of November 1945 we received orders to move back to Fort Devens, Massachusetts for processing. While there, classes were given on how to make an orderly transition to civilian life. The military made no effort to keep us from talking about anything we experienced. We were told to be calm for processing as many thousands were in the pipeline. During the height of the war it was estimated there were around 13 million in uniform. It took about three weeks to go through the system and finally I received my Honorable Discharge and returned to civilian life on 4 December 1945. For my service I was awarded the Combat Infantryman Badge, Good Conduct Medal, Victory Medal and several campaign ribbons. Some years later way after discharge I was notified and received the Bronze Star Medal as well as a Medal prepared only for Prisoners of War.

This is my story's ending. I have never gotten over the fact that of so many men that I have served with, seen so many die and how lucky I was to have gone through so much in a short time and survived to talk about my experiences. I must have been blessed, certainly very lucky and will be eternally grateful but will never forget how all this was brought upon me. Further blessings came forth a bit later as my two brothers were also phased out of the service and returned to us whole..

16

EPILOGUE

Was my story not important to tell? Was my experience of being shuffled around repeatedly and placed into a no win situation the norm for combat operations? Answers to these and other thoughts would probably never be known. Somehow, I could not bring myself to believe my experiences were similarly happening to other groups. If by some outside chance these happenings were expected, then wars should never be allowed to happen. When it was being done to me and my regiments ,although being a novice, somehow didn't seem to be right. This kind of experience certainly wasn't expressed in movies but possibly could be in print somewhere. Watching some of the war movies why would I not expect competent leadership? Difficult at best to find. Looking back, one has to wonder why our leaders find it so easy to start a war. Some historians and authors have described a slogan " Beware of the military and industrial complex" to describe their power to provoke a conflict and provide flowery rhetoric to justify it. Washington politics is easily swayed by "contributions" from the business community enabling this complex.

Why did I take so long to put my story together? Right after discharge and for many years later the agony of my experiences kept my bitterness ingrained for a long time. The early years after discharge left me with so much to cope with and adjusting took a while. Much still exists today and will carry with me till the end. My slow approach to writing this story is not that unusual. I guess I was just waiting for the right reason and at my age needed inspiration.. For example, the book about Prisoners of War " Hold at all costs" mentioned earlier was copyrighted in 2004 some 59 years after war's end. That book as noted did not contain my accounting of the war. Also, information about war statistics cited from the VFW magazine and mentioned in this story appeared in 1995.

My thinking may seem un American but I do love my country despite the words. What I have lost is faith in the quality and purpose of our leadership in Washington. Elected officials quickly forget their citizens and seem to address what's good for them. For me (and I hope many other Americans) our leaders will once and for all stop their missionary work to cure the world's ills, Why is our Government constantly trying to interfere with the internal affairs of foreign countries? Why must Washington think our form of Government is suitable for all countries? The notion that corporations and business are controlling foreign policy seems quite sound. I don't know if this will ever change but America should always be the first and only concern. Washington's power to start wars for little reason is cause for concern. Any change that may come won't help me but I fear for my children, grandchildren and the future young Americans.

In later years my body started to show the accumulating effects of time and certainly worsened from what I had to endure. Leg and circulation problems from the severe frostbite to my feet and lower limbs, tinnitus (ringing in the ears and other head noises) from combat and training noises, and other conditions from the poor nutrition during capture are now with me. I have for some time now been receiving medical services at a V.A. Hospital. The Veterans Administration considers me disabled due to my POW status with all problems being service connected. What I have are lingering problems progressing with age that will never go away and probably will worsen. As a veteran I have come to terms with my experience and moved on albeit with reduced bitterness. I know I will not get over this completely, but I will, as always, be an American.

Printed in the United States
By Bookmasters